# PLANT BASED PROTEIN SOURCES

THE ULTIMATE GUIDE TO HEALTHY EATING
WITH HIGH-PROTEIN FOODS AND RECIPES
FOR A PLANT-BASED DIET

## DEL GUNDRY

# DISCLAIMER

This book is not intended as a substitute for the medical advice of physicians. The reader should regularly consult a physician in matters relating to his/her health and particularly concerning any symptoms that may require diagnosis or medical attention.

No part of this book may be reproduced or transmitted in any form or by any means, electronic or mechanical, including photo-copying, recording or by any information storage and retrieval system, without written permission from the author.

The information provided within this book is for general informa-tional purposes only. While we try to keep the information up-to-date and correct, there are no representations or warranties, express or implied, about the completeness, accuracy, reliability, suitability or availability concerning the information, products, services, or related graphics contained in this book for any purpose. Any use of this infor-mation is at your own risk.

The methods described in this book are the author's thoughts. They are not intended to be a definitive set of instructions for this project. You may discover there are other methods and materials to accomplish the same result.

# CONTENTS

# INTRODUCTION

In the last few years, more and more individuals have developed an interest in complying with vegetarian or vegan diet regimens or minimizing their use of meat-based foods. A change from meat-based food is obtaining more nutrient and more easily available plant-based foods.

An individual might attempt a vegan diet plan for health and wellness purposes, for the well-being of animals and fight animal abuse, or for spiritual factors. In 2016, the Academy of Nutrition, and Dietetics, mentioned that a vegetarian or vegan diet regimen could supply all the dietary needs of grownups, kids, and even of expectant or breast-feeding women.

It is not uncommon that a suggestion to implement small changes fixes a selection of worldwide issues. Plant-based proteins as a substitution for meat is just one of those. Whether it is human health and wellness, animal environment, logging, or well-being adjustments (or every one of those) that worries you, switching to more plant-based sources of proteins can correlate to a basic (and delicious) method to address them.

This change, however, requires some alteration to how we

behave, pointing to waste and optimization of the use of plants healthy proteins. FReSH will certainly concentrate on the options that these organisations can bring, with a focus on healthy proteins.

However, obtaining sufficient healthy proteins and important nutrients can be harder for individuals that do not eat meat or animal-derived food. An individual has to prepare in advance to guarantee they obtain adequate healthy proteins, vitamins, iron, and calcium B-12, not as easily found in vegan diets differently form omnivorous diets containing meat, rich of these nutrients.

A usual worry concerning vegetarian and vegan diet regimens is that they may not have an adequate amount of healthy proteins intake.

Lots of specialists concur that a tactical vegetarian or vegan diet plan can supply you with all the nutrients you require. That stated, specific plant foods contain substantially much more healthy protein than others.

Higher-protein diet plans can lead to muscular tissue toughness, weight, and satiation loss.

Possibly, you have a clever pet and have decided you needed to go vegan. Possibly, you are reducing consuming beef to lighten your ecological impact. Whatever the factor, maybe when you minimize meat consumption in your diet regimen, obtaining adequate plant-based healthy protein comes to be essential.

Why? Every dish needs to have a number of healthy proteins, considering that it is what causes satiation (AKA stops overindulging), gives power, and assists the construction and the maintenance muscular tissue (particularly if you are a health club addict).

The bright side: Our food supply is currently full of plant-based healthy protein resources. Hemp seeds, and chia seeds, weren't resting on supermarket racks 5 years ago; neither were top-notch vegan healthy protein powders. We can currently satisfy our require-ments without chicken wings or hamburgers.

How is the healthiest feasible method to do that? Right here, there is whatever you require to find out about plant-based healthy protein.

The appeal of plant-based diet regimens has escalated, as an increasing number of individuals cut down on animal meat and loading their plates – and sustain their bodies – with primarily veggies and various sources of plant-based foods. That's a piece of excellent information for humans' health and wellness, along with that of stocks and the world.

# CHAPTER 1: WHAT IS A PLANT-BASED DIET?

The term "plant-based" explains a diet plan abundant in foods that originate from plants, preferably consumed not refined and "whole". A plant-based diet plan is comprised primarily of vegetables, fruits, beans, nuts, seeds, roots (potatoes, to name one), and grains. "Animal-based", on the other hand, describes a diet plan focused on animal itcms: meat, dairy products, eggs, and more.

Within the world of plant-based diet regimens, there are many different kinds. A vegetarian diet plan excludes meat (fowl, beef, pork, and all the others), fish and, shellfish. It, however, typically includes eggs and milk and milk-derived products (the term "lacto-ovo vegetarian" uses below). A "pescatarian" diet plan refers to a plant-based diet plan that additionally includes fish and/or fish and shell-fish, however, no meat is present.

Exactly, how do you obtain an adequate dose of healthy protein on a plant-based diet regimen?

This is an incredibly popular inquiry and a vital one. Yet, even if you aren't adhering to a plant-based diet plan, do you know how many healthy proteins you should be consuming daily?

Just how much healthy protein do we require?

Well, in the United States, the Dietary Reference Intake (DRI) for healthy protein is between 0.8 to 1.0 grams of healthy protein per kilo of body weight. Healthy protein is absolutely a vital nutrient, which plays several vital functions in the method our bodies work, however, we do not require significant amounts of it.

Lots of Americans eat almost twice the quantity of healthy protein needed. It is crucial to keep in mind that an excess of healthy protein cannot be stored in the body – eventually, its removal pressures the liver and kidneys. An extreme healthy protein intake is connected to specific cancers cells (i.e., colon, bust, prostate, pancreatic), kidney condition and, the weakening of bones. If you are taking in a selection of small, whole foods, you ought to obtain all the healthy protein you require, without straining your body.

# WHAT IS PROTEIN? AS WELL AS WHY DO I NEED IT?

Healthy protein is thought to be the foundation of life, considering that it is in every cell of the body.

Healthy protein is composed of amino acids that are connected to each other in lengthy chains. There are 20 different types of amino acids, and the series in which the various amino acids are set up aids to establish the duty of that specific healthy protein.

**Healthy proteins contribute to**

- Transferring particles throughout the body.
- Assisting the repair service of cells and making brand-new ones.
- Safeguarding the body from germs and infections.
- Provide appropriate development and growth in youngsters, young adults, and expectant females.

Without loading your diet plan with the proper quantities of healthy protein, you risk losing out on those crucial features. At some point, that can bring troubles, such as a loss of muscular tissue mass, that failing to expand, compromise the performance of the heart and lungs - leading to death.

# CHAPTER 2: WHY IS PROTEIN SO IMPORTANT?

As you might or might not understand, healthy proteins are made up of amino acids, called the "structure blocks" of life. Healthy protein assists create enzymes, hormonal agents, antibodies, and creating brand-new cells. The human body can make 9 of the 22 amino acids that make up healthy proteins.

## Arginine

Identified as a semi-essential or "conditionally" necessary amino acid, they rely on the developing phase and health and wellness condition of the person.

It can be found in: almonds, beetroots, Brazil nuts, buckwheat, carrots, cashews, celery, chickpeas, coconut, cucumbers, flaxseed, garlic, green veggies, hazelnuts, kidney beans, leeks, lentil, lettuce, dietary yeast, onion, parsnips, pecans, want nuts, potatoes, pumpkin seeds, radishes, sesame seeds, sprouts, sunflower seeds, and walnuts.

## Histidine

Particularly required throughout early stages for the correct development and growth – it used to be thought to be just important for infants, yet, it is currently recognized to be necessary for grownups.

It can be found in apples, bananas, beans, beetroots, buckwheat, carrots, melon, cauliflower, celery, citrus fruits, cucumber, dandelion, endive, garlic, eco-friendlies, beans, mushrooms, pomegranates, radish, rice, algae, sesame, spirulina, spinach, and turnip.

## Isoleucine

Essential for muscle mass upkeep, manufacturing, and healing – particularly post-workout. It is associated with hemoglobin development, the management of blood sugar levels, embolism's development, and power.

It can be found in almonds, avocados, cashews, chickpeas, coconut, lentils, olives, papaya, algae, and most seeds like sunflower.

## Leucine

Necessary for development hormonal agent manufacturing, cell manufacturing, and repair service, it stops muscle mass loss. It is used when dealing with problems such as Parkinson's condition.

It can be found in almonds, asparagus, avocados, chickpeas, coconut, lentils, oats, olives, papayas, rice, sunflower seeds, and walnuts.

## Lysine

Great for calcium absorption, bone growth, nitrogen upkeep, cell repair work, hormonal agent manufacturing, antibody manufacturing.

It can be found in amaranth, apples, apricots, beans, beetroots, carrots, celery, cucumber, dandelion eco-friendlies, grapes, papayas, parsley, pears, peas, spinach, and turnip eco-friendlies.

## Methionine

It is described as the "cleaner" – essential for fat emulsification, food digestion, anti-oxidant (cancer cells avoidance), arterial plaque avoidance (heart wellness), and heavy metal elimination.

It can be found in black beans, Brazil nuts, cashews, kidney beans, oats, sesame seeds, spirulina, spinach, sunflower seeds, and watercress.

## Phenylalanine

A forerunner for tyrosine and the indicating particles of dopamine, norepinephrine (noradrenaline), and epinephrine (adrenaline), in addition, a forerunner to the skin pigment: melanin. Sustains understanding and memory, mind procedures, and altitude perception.

It can be found in apples, beetroots, carrots, cashews, flaxseed, hazelnuts, dietary yeast, parsley, pineapples, pumpkin seeds, sesame seeds, sunflower seeds, spinach, and tomatoes.

## Threonine

Screens physical healthy proteins for their preservation or reuse.

It can be found in almonds, beans, carrots, celery, chickpeas, collards, flaxseed, eco-friendlies, green leafy veggies, kale, lentils, lima beans, nori, nuts, papayas, sesame seeds, sunflower seeds, and walnuts.

## Tryptophan

It is required for niacin and serotonin manufacturing, discomfort perception, and monitoring of the rest of the body.

It can be found in Brussels sprouts, carrots, celery, chives, dandelion eco-friendlies, endive, fennel, dietary yeast, pumpkin seeds, sesame seeds, break beans, spinach, sunflower seeds, walnuts, and turnips.

## Valine

Aids muscular tissue manufacturing, healing, strength, endurance - balance nitrogen degrees, and it is utilized in the therapy of alcohol-related mental retardation.

It can be found in apples, almonds, bananas, beetroots, broccoli, carrots, celery, dandelion environment-friendlies, lettuce, dietary yeast, okra, parsley, parsnips, pomegranates, potatoes, squash, turnips, and tomatoes.

Within the world of plant-based diet regimens, there are a lot of different kinds. A vegetarian diet plan excludes meat (fowl, beef, pork, and all the others), fish and, shellfish. It, however, typically includes eggs and milk and milk-derived products (the term "lacto-ovo vegetarian" uses below). A "pescatarian" diet plan refers to a plant-based diet plan that additionally includes fish and/or fish and shellfish, however, no meat is present.

# CAN AID WEIGHT LOSS AND PREVENT WEIGHT GAIN

When it comes to losing weight, healthy protein is exceptionally vital.

As you understand, you require the consumption of fewer calories than you burn to slim down.

Scientific researches well sustain that consuming healthy protein can enhance the number of calories you lose weight by increasing your metabolic rate (calories out) and decreasing your hunger (calories in).

Healthy protein at around 25-30% of the complete everyday calories has been revealed to enhance the metabolic rate by as much as 80-100 calories each day, opposed to the usual reduced healthy protein diet regimens.

Most likely, the essential benefit of healthy protein to weight loss is its capacity to decrease hunger and trigger a spontaneous decrease in calorie consumption. Healthy protein keeps you feeling satiated better than both fats and carbohydrates.

One research in overweight men revealed that healthy protein at an amount of 25% of calories consumed, enhanced the sensations of feeling full, lowered the need for late-night snacking by fifty percent, and minimized compulsive thoughts regarding food by 60%.

In one more research study, females that raised their healthy protein consumption to 30% of calories wound up eating 441 fewer calories each day and shed 11 extra pounds in 12 weeks - merely by including extra healthy protein to their diet regimen.

Healthy protein does not just assist you shedding weight, it can prevent you from gaining weight in the first place.

In one research, a moderate boost in healthy protein from 15% to 18% of calories minimized the number of fat individuals gained back after weight-loss by 50%.

A high healthy protein consumption, additionally, aids you in maintaining and developing muscular tissue mass, which burns a handful of calories all the time.

Consuming a lot of healthy protein makes it easier to adhere to any weight management diet plan – be it high-carb, low-carb, or something in between.

According to these research studies, a healthy protein consumption, of around 30% of the total calories, might be optimum for fat burning. It enhances your metabolic rate and triggers a spontaneous decrease in calorie consumption. This totals up to 150 grams daily for a person on a 2000-calorie diet regimen.

You can determine it by increasing your calorie consumption by 0.075.

# CAN HELP YOU GAIN MUSCLE AS WELL AS STRENGTH

Muscular tissues are mainly constructed of healthy protein.

Just like a lot of cells in your body, muscular tissues are vibrant and continuously being broken down and rebuilt.

To gain muscle mass, your body must manufacture much more muscle mass with healthy protein than it breaks down.

To put it simply, there requires to be a net positive, healthy protein equilibrium in your body – frequently called nitrogen equilibrium, as healthy protein is high in nitrogen.

Because of this, individuals that desire a lot of muscle mass require to consume a higher quantity of healthy protein (and lift weights, obviously). It is well recorded that a greater healthy protein consumption assists in constructing muscle mass and toughness.

Individuals that wish to maintain the muscular tissue they've already gained might require to raise their healthy protein consumption when shedding body fat, as a high healthy protein consumption can aid protect against muscle mass loss that typically happens during a weight loss.

Researches typically do not look at the portion of calories, however, they look at the daily grams of healthy protein per kgs or extra pounds of body weight when it comes to muscular tissue mass.

A typical suggestion for gaining muscle mass is 1 gram of healthy protein per extra pound of body weight or 2.2 grams of healthy protein per kg.

Various other researchers have approximated the healthy protein amount requires to be a minimum of 0.7 grams per extra pound or 1.6 grams per kg.

Countless researches have attempted to establish the ideal quantity of healthy protein for muscle mass gain; however, they could not converge to a single verdict.

Some researches reveal that a greater intake than 0.8 grams per extra pound (1.8 grams per kg) has no advantage, while others suggest that the consumption of more than 1 gram of healthy protein per extra pound (2.2 grams per kg) is the best.

It is difficult to offer specific numbers due to contrasting research outcomes, however, 0.7 – 1 gram per extra pound (1.6 - 2.2 grams per kg) of body weight appears to be a reasonable range.

If you have an abundance of body fat, making use of either your lean mass or your objective weight, as opposed to your complete body weight, is a great concept, as it is mainly your lean mass that identifies the quantity of healthy protein you require.

If you desire to preserve and/or gain muscle mass, it is vital to consume an adequate amount of healthy protein. The majority of researches recommend that 0.7 - 1 gram per extra pound of lean mass (1.6 - 2.2 grams per kg) suffice.


**Various other circumstances that can increase protein needs**

Ignoring for a moment muscular tissue mass and body objectives, individuals that are more energetic, do require even more healthy protein than individuals that are less active.

If your work is requiring you to constantly stroll around, run, do kind of swimming or workout, you require to consume even more healthy protein.

Endurance professional athletes, likewise, require substantial quantities of healthy protein – about 0.5-0.65 grams per extra pound, or 1.2-1.4 grams per kg.

Older generations have a raised amount of healthy protein required - approximately 50% more than the DRI, or about 0.45-0.6 grams per extra pound (1-1.3 grams per kg) of body weight.

This can aid stop the weakening of bones and sarcopenia (decrease in muscular tissue mass), both substantial issues in seniors.

Individuals recuperating from injuries might additionally require even more healthy protein.

Healthy protein demands have substantially been boosted by all those individuals that are energetic, in addition to that, older individuals and adults receive beneficial results as healthy proteins help to recuperate from injuries.

# CHAPTER 3: HOW TO CALCULATE PROTEIN RDA BEST FOR YOUR BODY

Healthy protein is a vital nutrient; its intake is essential for the wellness of your muscle mass and, for the wellness of the heart. Consuming healthy protein can, also, aid you handle specific illness and sustain your weight-loss initiatives. The quantity of healthy protein you need to take in is based upon your weight, exercise, age and various other variables.

# THE RDA FOR PROTEIN

The Recommended Dietary Allowance, or RDA, for healthy protein is based on your weight. Most individuals ought to take in 0.8 grams of healthy protein per kilo of body weight. Aspects such as whether you are a professional athlete or are an expectant woman can additionally play an important factor in your healthy protein consumption.

Individuals can eat up to 2 grams of healthy protein per kilo of bodyweight without long-term consequences. According to a 2016 evaluation post in the Journal of Food Functionality, the bearable limitation of healthy protein intake is 3.5 grams per kilo of body weight: it is basically more than 4 times than the basic amount that the RDA suggests for healthy protein. Extreme healthy protein consumption over a long-term period might impact the gastrointestinal, kidneys or vascular wellness.

# COMPUTING THE RDA FOR PROTEIN

To figure out just how much healthy protein you ought to be consuming, there is a simple formula: take your weight, which you most likely recognize in extra pounds, and then you need to transform it to kgs. The ordinary American male evaluates to have 195.7 extra pounds (matching approximately 88.77 kilos), while the typical American woman evaluates to have 168.5 extra pounds (which amounts to a concerning 75.21 kilos).

Considering that most individuals need to consume about 0.8 grams of healthy protein per kilo of body weight, this implies that the RDA formula is:

- (0.8 grams of healthy protein) x (weight in kilos).

Provided this standard, many males should consider that they should have an intake of 71 grams of healthy protein daily, due to the fact that 0.8 x 88.77 = 71.016. Ladies should eat around 60 grams of healthy protein each day, considering that the equation gives 0.8 x 75.21 = 60.168.

You can additionally simply increase your weight in extra pounds by 0.36 grams of healthy protein if you are having problem computing your body weight in kilos. This would change the RDA formula to the following:

- (0.36 grams of healthy protein) x (weight in extra pounds).

There is a selection of healthy protein consumption calculators offered online if you are not comfortable in computing your RDA for healthy protein by hand. You can use sites like the "United States Department of Agriculture's Dietary Reference Intakes Calculator".

# INDIVIDUALS WHO NEED MORE PROTEIN

The RDA for healthy protein usually is 0.8 gram per kilo of body weight, lots of individuals can take in extra healthy protein safely. Professional athletes, for example, can eat as much of healthy protein as they desire as they burn a lot by exercising. Other individuals, like expecting females, nursing mothers and older generations additionally require eating even more of this nutrient.

The quantity of healthy protein you ought to eat as a professional athlete relies on the sort of exercise you take part in. Generally, individuals carrying out different workout routines ought to eat:

- Minimum exercise (periodic stroll or extending): 1.0 gram of healthy protein per kilo of body weight.
- Modest exercise (regular weight-lifting, quick strolling): 1.3 grams of healthy protein per kg of body weight.
- Extreme training (professional athletes, routine joggers): 1.6 grams of healthy protein per kilo of body weight.

Expectant ladies, likewise, require eating even more healthy protein than the standard suggested. According to a 2016 research in the Journal of Advances in Nutrition, women need to take in between 1.2 and 1.52 grams of healthy protein per kilo of weight every day while pregnant.

The reduced quantity (1.2 grams) is appropriate for very early maternities stages of around 16 weeks, while the top quantity is advised for later maternities of about 36 weeks. The assumption of healthy protein by expectant ladies isn't just crucial for the development of the fetus; it is additionally vital in assisting the mothers' body prepare to nurse their kids.

# CHAPTER 4: HOW TO CALCULATE YOUR PROTEIN NEEDS

It is crucial that we consume a sufficient amount of healthy protein each day to cover our body's requirements. Do you recognize just how much healthy protein you require?

Numerous professional athletes and other people that work out a lot assume that they ought to enhance their healthy protein consumption to assist them to shed their weight or construct even more muscle mass. It is real that the extra you work out, the higher your healthy protein requirement will undoubtedly be.

# HEALTHY PROTEIN INTAKE GUIDELINES

Healthy proteins are the standard foundation of the body. They are comprised of amino acids and are required for the formation of muscular tissues, blood, skin, hair, nails, and the wellbeing of the interior body's organs. Besides water, healthy protein is one of the most abundant compounds in the body, and the majority of it is in the skeletal muscle mass.

Considering this, it is assuring to understand that according to the Dietary Guidelines for Americans between 2015-2020, most individuals obtain sufficient healthy protein daily. The very same record directs out that the consumption of fish and shellfish, and plant-based proteins such as seeds and nuts, are frequently lacking.

If you are an athlete, nonetheless, your healthy protein requirements might be somewhat greater considering that resistance training and endurance exercises can swiftly break down muscular tissue healthy protein.

The basic standards for strength-trained and endurance professional athletes, according to the Academy of Nutrition and Dietetics, Dietitians of Canada, and the American College of Sports Medicine, is the recommended amount laying in between 1.2 and 2 grams of healthy protein per kg of body weight to achieve maximum efficiency and the health and wellness of the body.

If you are attempting to gain even more muscular tissue, you might assume that you require a lot more healthy protein, yet this isn't what you should do. There is proof that very strict professional athletes or exercisers might take in even more healthy protein (over 3 grams/kilograms daily), but for the typical exerciser, consumption of as much as 2 grams/per kg daily suffices for building muscle mass.

# VARIOUS WAYS TO DETERMINE PROTEIN NEEDS

When establishing your healthy protein requirements, you can either recognize a percent of overall day-to-day calories, or you can target in detail the number of grams of healthy protein to eat each day.

*Percent of daily calories*

Present USDA nutritional standards recommend that adult males and females should take an amount in between 10 and 35 percent of their overall calories intake from healthy protein. To obtain your number and to track your consumption, you'll require to understand the number of calories you eat daily.

To keep a healthy and balanced weight, you need to take in about the same variety of calories that you burn daily.

Just increase that number by 10 percent and by 35 percent to obtain your variety when you understand precisely how many calories you take in daily.

As an example, a male that eats 2,000 calories each day would more or less require to eat between 200 to 700 calories every day of healthy protein.

*Healthy protein grams each day*

As an option to the portion method, you can target the specific amount of healthy protein grams each day.

One straightforward method to obtain an amount of healthy protein grams daily is to equate the percent array into a particular healthy protein gram variety. The mathematical formula for this is very easy.

Each gram of healthy protein consists of 4 calories, so you will just need to split both calorie array numbers by 4.

A guy that consumes 2,000 calories daily must take in between 200 and 700 calories from healthy protein or 50 to 175 grams of healthy protein.

There are various other methods to obtain a much more specific number which might consider lean muscular tissue mass and/or exercise degree.

You can establish your fundamental healthy protein requirement as a percent of your complete day-to-day calorie consumption or as a series of healthy protein grams daily.

*Healthy protein needs based on weight and activity*

The ordinary adult demands a minimum of 0.8 grams of healthy protein per kg of body weight each day. One kg equates to 2.2 extra pounds, so an individual that has 165 extra pounds or 75 kg would more or less require around 60 grams of healthy protein daily.

Your healthy protein requirements might raise if you are very active. The Academy of Nutrition and Dietetics, American College of Sports Medicine and the Dietitians of Canada, recommend that professional athletes require even more healthy protein.

They recommend that endurance professional athletes (those that often take part in sports like running, biking, or swimming) take in 1.2 to 1.4 grams of healthy protein per kilo of body weight daily which equates to 0.5 to 0.6 grams of healthy protein per extra pound of body weight.

The companies recommend that strength-trained professional athletes (that engage in exercises like powerlifting or weightlifting often) take in 1.6 to 1.7 grams of healthy protein per kg of body weight. This equates to 0.7 to 0.8 grams of healthy protein per extra pound of body weight.

*Healthy protein needs based on lean body mass*

A new approach of finding out how much healthy protein you require is focused on the degree of the exercise (how much energy you spend) and your lean body mass. Some professionals really feel that this is an exact extra method because our lean body mass needs extra healthy protein for upkeep than fat.

Lean body mass (LBM) is merely the quantity of bodyweight that is not fat. There are various methods to identify your lean body mass, yet the most convenient is to deduct your body fat from your overall body mass.

You'll require to establish your body fat percent. There are various methods to obtain the number of your body fat consisting of screening with skin calipers, BIA ranges, or DEXA scans. You can approximate your body fat with the following calculating formula.

To determine your overall body fat in extra pounds, you will need to increase your body weight by the body fat portion. If you evaluate yourself to be 150 pounds and that your fat percent is 30, then 45 of those bodyweight pounds would certainly be fat (150 x 30% = 45).

Compute lean body mass. Merely deduct your body fat weight from your overall body weight. Utilizing the exact same instance, the lean body mass would certainly be 105 (150 - 45 = 105).

# CALCULATING YOUR PROTEIN NEEDS

While the above standards offer you a general idea of where your healthy protein consumption needs to drop, determining the quantity of day-to-day healthy protein that's right for you, there is another method that can assist you in tweaking the previous results.

To identify your healthy protein requirements in grams (g), you need to initially determine your weight in kgs (kg) by separating your weight in pounds by 2.2.

Next off, choose the number of grams of healthy protein per kilo of bodyweight that is appropriate for you.

Use the reduced end of the array (0.8 g per kg) if you consider yourself to be healthy but not very active.

You should intake a more significant amount of protein (in between 1.2 and 2.0) if you are under tension, expecting, recuperating from a health problem, or if you are associated with extreme and constant weight or endurance training.

(You might require the recommendations of a physician or nutritional expert to assist you to establish this number).

Increase your weight in kg times the number of healthy protein grams per day.

*For instance:*

A 154 pound man that has as a routine exercising and lifting weights, but is not training at an elite degree:

154 lb/2.2 = 70 kg.

70 kg x 1.7 = 119 grams healthy protein each day.

*Healthy protein as a percent of complete calories*

An additional means to determine how much healthy protein you require is utilizing your everyday calorie consumption and the percentage of calories that will certainly originate from healthy protein.

Figure out exactly how many calories your body requires each day to keep your current weight.

Discover what your basic metabolic rate (BMR) is by utilizing a BMR calculator (often described as a basic power expense, or BEE, calculator).

Figure out the amount of calories you burn via day-to-day tasks and include that number to your BMR.

Next off, choose what portion of your diet plan will certainly originate from healthy protein. The percent you pick will certainly be based upon your objectives, physical fitness degree, age, type of body, and your metabolic rate. The Dietary Guidelines for Americans 2015-2020 advises that healthy protein represent something in between 10 percent and 35 percent for grownups suggested caloric intake.

Multiply that percentage by the complete variety of calories your body requires for the day to establish overall everyday calories from healthy protein.

Split that number by 4. (Quick Reference - 4 calories = 1 gram of healthy protein.)

*For instance:*

A 140-pound woman that eats 1800 calories each day consuming a diet plan having 20 percent of the total caloric intake consisting of healthy protein:

1800 x 0.20 = 360 calories from healthy protein.

360 calories/ 4 = 90 grams of healthy protein each day.

*Compute daily protein need*

To establish your day-to-day healthy protein requirement, increase your LBM by the suitable task degree.

- Less active (normally non-active): increase by 0.5.
- Light task (consists of strolling or horticulture): increase by 0.6.
- Modest (30 mins of a modest task, thrice weekly): increase by 0.7.
- Energetic (one hr of workout, 5 times regular): increase by 0.8.
- Really energetic (10 to 20 hrs of regular workout): increase by 0.9.
- Professional athlete (over 20 hrs of regular workout): increase by 1.0.

Based upon this approach, a 150-pound individual with an LBM of 105 would certainly need a day-to-day healthy protein amount that varies between 53 grams (if inactive) to 120 grams (if very active).

# HOW MANY GRAMS OF PROTEIN SHOULD YOU EAT PER KILOGRAM OF BODY WEIGHT?

The quantity of healthy protein you take in is essential for your wellness. Lots of people ought to take in 0.8 grams of healthy protein per kilo of body weight, however, this quantity can alter based upon different elements. Individuals that are expecting, lactating, that have particular health and wellness problems or that are extremely energetic, commonly need even more healthy protein than the standard.

*Healthy protein requirement per kilogram*

You need to recognize your healthy protein demand per kg of body weight. Basically, the Recommended Dietary Allowance or RDA for healthy protein is 0.8 gram per kg of body weight.

Specific diet plans, like low-carbohydrate diet plans or the Atkins diet and even paleo diet regimens, might need you to eat even more healthy protein than this while still permitting you to take in a well-balanced diet regimen. Various other diet plans, like the Dukan diet or the predator diet regimen, concentrate on consuming only healthy protein and fat.

Raising the quantity of healthy protein you consume can be

healthy and balanced and excellent, mainly if the healthy protein you are eating is originating from different resources. However, according to the Harvard Medical School, taking in even more than 2 grams of healthy protein per kg of body weight or even more can be harmful to your wellness.

According to the Centers for Disease Control, the ordinary American male values 195.7 extra pounds (or 88.77 kilos), while the typical American lady values 168.5 extra pounds (or 75.21 kilos). Given that the RDA is 0.8 grams of healthy protein for every single kilo of body weight, this indicates that a lot of males need to take in about 71 grams of healthy protein daily. Females that are a bit smaller sized ought to generally take in around 60 grams of healthy protein each day.

# CHAPTER 5: HEALTH BENEFITS OF PROTEIN

Healthy protein assists to maintain body cells healthy, consisting of muscular tissues, body organs, nerve system, skin, blood, and hair. It additionally functions as a transportation system for oxygen, minerals, vitamins, and fats.

Additionally, consuming healthy protein can assist you in managing your weight since it takes longer to absorb a protein-rich meal. After taking in a meal with healthy protein, you are most likely to feel completely satisfied and full for much longer.

Some healthy protein foods have extra health and wellness advantages. Fish, such as salmon, tuna, herring, and trout, are high in healthy protein and additionally omega-3 fats that are important for the general health and wellness of the body. Legumes are high in healthy protein, and they're high in fiber; they are rich in phytochemicals that might have wellness advantages.

# SHORTAGE

Unlike fat and sugar, our body has little ability to store healthy protein. Your body would undoubtedly begin to damage down muscular tissue if you were to quit consuming healthy protein.

Healthy protein shortage is uncommon in established nations, nevertheless, it can take place if you are not eating enough nutrient-dense food every day.

# OVERCONSUMPTION

On the other side, it is feasible to consume excessive healthy protein. Some individuals think that excess healthy protein is secreted in pee; nonetheless, just part of the healthy protein is eliminated. An additional part of the healthy protein is transformed into sugar for power or saved as fat.

If you consume too much healthy protein – and several calories as an outcome – you run the risk of gaining weight from excess calorie intake.

You are most likely not obtaining adequate carb or fat for your body to work appropriately if your calorie objective remains on track however, you obtain even more healthy protein than you require. The trick to having correct nutrition is accomplishing the right equilibrium of macronutrients.

Consuming huge quantities of healthy protein can lead to dehydration in elite professional athletes. If you comply with a high healthy protein diet regimen, it is crucial to drink plenty of water.

# EXCESS CONSUMPTION OF PROTEIN

It is entirely appropriate to boost the quantity of healthy protein you consume, yet, there are, obviously, restrictions to the amount you need to eat. According to the Harvard Medical School, consuming 2 grams of healthy protein per kg of body weight or even more could be poor for your wellness. Several of the downsides that can take place when eating way too much healthy protein consist of:

- High cholesterol, commonly related to the intake of excessive hydrogenated fat, which is in animal-derived foods and various other edible items like coconuts.
- Gastrointestinal system concerns, consisting of looseness of the bowels and irregular bowel movements.
- Kidney troubles, consisting of kidney rocks and other kidney conditions.
- Increased risks of age-related conditions, consisting of cardiovascular diseases and the formation of cancer cells.
- Weight gain.

Consuming huge quantities of healthy protein over a brief

amount of time most likely will not impact you in these ways. Long-lasting adherence to a high-protein diet plan might adversely affect your wellness.

It is vital to make sure that you are still consuming a well-balanced diet regimen if you choose to take in a significant quantity of healthy protein each day. In this situation, that would certainly indicate picking various kinds of healthy protein, like fatty fish, eggs and plant-based proteins, in addition to animal-derived products. Taking in a range of healthy proteins will certainly assist enhance the number of nutrients in your diet regimen, decrease the quantity of hydrogenated fat you are eating and make you far better off in regards to your total wellness.

# CONSUMING TOO LITTLE PROTEIN

Taking in too little healthy protein is simply as bad as taking in too much over lengthy durations of time. Individuals that take in little quantities of healthy protein might merely by sticking to vegetarian, various other diets or vegan diet regimens that include many plant-based foods.

You must realize that a healthy protein consumption of less than 5 percent, can trigger loss of muscular tissue mass. It is thought that too little proteins in the system are insufficient to maintain a healthy living standard. Low-fat, low-protein, high-carbohydrate diet plans include eating a minimum of this much healthy protein.

You can use the United States Department of Agriculture Dietary Reference Intakes Calculator if you desire to make sure that you are obtaining the best quantity of healthy protein each day. This device will certainly not just reveal you how much healthy protein to consume, but also the quantities of all the nutrients you ought to eat to preserve excellent general health and wellness. Nowadays, several apps are likewise readily available to aid you to figure out the quantity of healthy protein that's appropriate for you, no matter whether you are attempting to slim down, gaining muscle mass or simply remain healthy and balanced.

# DOES PROTEIN HAVE ANY NEGATIVE HEALTH EFFECTS?

Healthy protein has been unjustly criticized for a variety of illnesses.

Some individuals think that a high-protein diet plan can cause kidney damages and the weakening of bones. However, these claims are not sustained by scientific researches.

Healthy protein limitation is useful for individuals with pre-existing kidney problems, but healthy protein has never been revealed to trigger kidney damages in healthy and balanced individuals.

A higher intake of healthy protein consumption has been discovered to reduce blood pressure and assist in combating diabetes mellitus, which are two of the major threat variables for kidney illnesses. Anyway, any possible risks of people who adopt a healthy protein diet are debunked by all the favorable results generated by these elements.

Healthy protein has additionally been criticized for the weakening of bones, which appears weird if you think that there are researches that reveal that it can prevent and cure this problem.

Generally, there is no proof that a fairly high healthy protein consumption has any kind of negative impact on healthy and balanced individuals attempting to remain healthy and balanced.

Healthy protein does not have any kind of adverse impact on kidneys in healthy and balanced individuals, also, researches reveal that it brings enhanced benefits to bone wellness.

# CHAPTER 6: HERE'S A LOOK AT SPECIFIC FACTORS THAT IMPACT YOUR PROTEIN NEEDS:

Because healthy protein isn't one-size-fits-all, there are particular groups that require even more and might have a more challenging time obtaining a sufficient amount of protein.

**Are you a vegetarian or vegan?**

Excellent information for those giving up meat-based foods: if you are consuming sufficient calories, selecting a plant-based diet regimen does not immediately indicate you are not eating sufficient healthy protein. According to the Academy of Nutrition and Dietetics, the terms "full" and "insufficient" healthy protein are deceiving. "Protein from a selection of plant foods, consumed throughout the training course of a day, materials sufficient of all essential (necessary) amino acids when calorie needs are fulfilled," the Academy claimed in a 2016 placement declaration.

Vegans, and vegetarians, might require to pay a little more focus to what foods provide to assure they get the very best protein-for-calorie worth. It is harder for them than ordinary meat-eaters. However, consuming a different diet plan that consists of protein-rich vegetables and soy will undoubtedly maintain your body and muscle mass just fine.

Healthy protein isn't simply an issue for the shake-guzzling body-builder intending to develop muscle - or the elite runner attempting to maintain it. Sufficient healthy protein is required in all degrees of physical fitness and the capacity to sustain the development of muscular tissue and functions as a foundation.

The IOM's standards were based upon research studies in inactive people. The American College of Sports Medicine, and the International Society of Sports Nutrition, suggest going for even more healthy protein if you are energetic, as much as 2 grams/kilogram of body weight daily to preserve muscular tissue mass. While maintaining healthy protein within 10 to 35 percent of your daily calories still is correct, professionals suggest eating 15 to 25 grams of healthy protein within an hour post-workout (an instance is 1 cup of milk, 1 ounce almonds and 5 dried out apricots) to optimize outcomes.

Does even more healthy protein equivalent far better outcomes? Not so, states an existing study, which recommends that advantages level off after suggested consumption. "It is kind of like including washing cleaning agent to your clothes - it is not going to get them cleaner - but having the correct amount, at the correct time, is essential," Crandall claims.

Foods high in a particular amino acid-the foundation of protein - called leucine - might be most reliable for the upkeep, repair work and the development of muscle mass. High-leucine foods are, for example, milk, soybeans, salmon, beef, hen, eggs and nuts like peanuts. While you need to aim to satisfy your healthy protein needs from food, whey healthy protein supplements are additionally high in leucine and are a research-backed alternative.

**Are you over 65?**

As we age, our bodies end up being much less effective at

changing the healthy protein we eat into brand-new muscle mass. The outcome is steady muscular tissue loss that can cause lowered resilience, frailty and loss of movement. You can offer "Father Time" a one-two strike by keeping eating energetic and sufficient healthy protein-dense food.

Two worldwide study halls advise that older people should consume the same amount of proteins as young professional athletes: keep your minimum everyday healthy protein consumption to 1 gram/kilogram of body weight (68 grams and 80 grams for a 180-pound male and a 150-pound female, respectively).

They have expanded your protein intake - about 25 to 30 grams of healthy protein at each meal - since the quantity of healthy protein required to set off muscular tissue upkeep is greater. According to research published by the Journal of Clinical Nutrition, males and females aged 67 to 84 that consumed more healthy proteins and had more health benefits over 2 years resulted in having extra muscular tissue than those that failed.

**Are you pregnant or breastfeeding?**

"Protein requires to be increased by a minimum of 10 grams daily throughout the 3rd and 2nd trimesters because your infant is growing - and thus it requires the means to grow," states Rachel Brandeis MS, RDN, that concentrates on maternity nutrition. The IOM suggests that expecting ladies should consume a minimum of 1.1 grams/kilogram of body weight daily or around 70 grams in total.

The current study recommends that during the entire maternity period healthy protein requirements might be somewhat greater than these previous numbers, nonetheless, it is ideal to sign in with a physician or signed up dietitian to see just how much healthy protein is right for you.

When it comes to nursing mothers, your body will certainly require extra calories and healthy protein to produce an adequate amount of milk.

Healthy protein is a vital nutrient, and when you are consuming a diverse, healthy and balanced diet regimen, you are most likely obtaining a sufficient amount. Objective to consist of protein-rich foods throughout your day, not simply at supper. If you are an individual that requires even more protein - whether you are energetic, older or pregnant - you might need to be extra aware of your healthy protein consumption to make sure you are obtaining what you require.

# CHAPTER 7: PLANT-BASED PROTEIN

Legumes, nuts, and seeds are excellent resources of healthy protein. Some veggies (such as spinach or kale) and grains (such as quinoa) additionally supply healthy protein in smaller percentages.

To maintain your healthy proteins from plant-derived food healthy and balanced, you should select recipes and cooking approaches that protect their dietary advantages - using tofu as a substitute for meat in a stir-fry, including seeds or nuts to a supper salad, or making use of completely dry beans like kidney-shaped beans, navy or black beans as your essential healthy protein resource for a couple of dishes.

# WHY YOU MUST CONSUME PLANT-BASED HEALTHY PROTEIN

Healthy protein plays numerous crucial functions in the body, so it is essential to obtain a sufficient amount of them. (How much you require relies on your age, sex, task and weight.) Plant healthy protein can be an excellent choice in contrast to healthy animal protein. Below there are a couple of reasons that explain that.

## 1. Plant healthy proteins are full, healthy proteins

There's a preferred false impression that healthy plant protein is substandard to healthy animal protein, yet, that's not the case. You do not need to consume meat to obtain ample quantities of healthy protein.

Healthy animal protein usually has more healthy protein per offering than vegetables. It is commonly thought to be a total healthy protein because it includes all the 9 necessary amino acids that our bodies cannot make by itself. Due to the fact that we require to obtain them from our diet plan; our body produces the others that we need. These amino acids are called crucial. Numerous plant foods do not include all the 9 vital amino acids and are occasionally described as insufficient healthy protein.

Amino acids are the structure blocks of healthy protein, and in general, we require sufficient quantities for the body to operate. As long as we consume a range of foods over our days that jointly have all of the vital amino acids, the body has the raw product it requires to make healthy proteins.

That stated some plant foods are taken into consideration full, healthy proteins - spirulina, chia seeds and maca powder, among others.

## 2. Plant healthy protein is a lot more lasting

When picking what to place in our mouths, we should take notice that environmental changes and the decreasing of all-natural sources make it much more essential than ever before to be careful of the wellness of the earth.

It is clear that our food system is a significant motorist of environment adjustment, air pollution, and the exhaustion of natural deposits - professionals have discovered that as much as 75 percent of complete farming exhausts originate from generating animal-based food. Without committed initiatives and technical steps to minimize this problem, our food system's effect will just become worse, making our atmosphere uninhabitable and risky.

On a serious notice, however, the future isn't completely grim as we could expect - making the change towards a much healthier, plant-based diet regimens is a vital component of the service. Healthy plant protein is extra effective and much less resource-intensive to generate than healthy animal protein, making it the premium option in terms of sustainability.

## 3. Plant healthy protein sustains healthiness

Healthy plant-derived protein tends to be high in vitamins,

minerals, fiber, antioxidants and various other substances that we require to remain healthy and balanced. Some kinds include considerable quantities of healthy and balanced fats, as well. Beans, nuts, seeds and entire groups of grains are all healthy plant proteins that you should consume.

Research studies have revealed that healthy plant protein, as part of a plant-based diet plan, lowered the body weight and enhanced insulin resistance in obese individuals. If you are looking to reach your healthy and balanced weight, including even more plants to your diet plan is a terrific step, to begin with.

Extra research studies have established that plant-based diet plans might decrease high blood pressure, cholesterol levels and body mass index, and minimize the risk of stroke and cardiovascular diseases. In people with Type 2 diabetic issues, a plant-based diet plan has been discovered to assist the management of blood sugar levels. An added study has revealed that an extra plant-based diet regimen might reduce the risk of creating diabetic issues.

This is a piece of motivating information for individuals currently managing several of the following problems: patients being treated for persistent illness and heart problems that consume a plant-based diet plan might not require as numerous drugs. For healthy and balanced individuals, plant-based diet plans have been connected with a lowered danger of all-cause death amongst United States adults. Thinking about all the advantages, it is understandable why medical professionals and specialized nutritionists are suggesting a plant-based diet regimen to the majority of their clients.

## 4. Plant healthy protein is kinder to animals

Ninety-five percent of stocks in the U.S. are elevated on agriculture, according to the ASPCA. These dismal, contaminated commercial ranches, created to fulfil the need for meat and various other animal-based foods, have brought on an unknown quantity of animal ruthlessness and suffering.

While an enhancing variety of meat and dairy products businesses are functioning to enhance problems for their animals, very little regulation remains in the area to maintain animals risk-free. There are no government regulations to secure animals on ranches, and states that have anti-cruelty regulations hardly ever implement them.

The straightforward truth of the issue is that consuming even more plants suggests (we would certainly assume) consuming fewer animal products, which is much better for your wellbeing, for the wellbeing of the earth, and definitely of the one of the animals.

## 5. Plant healthy protein is affordable

A plant-based diet plan does not need to cost a fortune. On the other hand, plant healthy protein can be unbelievably budget-friendly.

Peas, beans and lentils are one of the most inexpensive and most versatile, recipe-friendly resources of plant healthy protein. Various other choices that set you back a little bit, yet, are really high in healthy protein (seeds and nuts, as an example) can still be a good value, specifically if you purchase them wholesale. They additionally give high fats, together with various other essential nutrients, providing you much more value.

# CHAPTER 8: WAYS TO GET PROTEIN WHEN YOU'RE ON A PLANT-BASED DIET

I want to keep things straight in this book. As opposed to common belief, it is not just feasible to enhance your health and wellness on a plant-based diet plan; when done right, I really suggest it.

# WHERE DO YOU OBTAIN YOUR HEALTHY PROTEIN?

Think it or not, you can really prosper, and never ever endure a healthy protein shortage on a plant-based diet. Since you should consider precisely how energetic your way of living is, a well-thought whole food plant-based diet regimen offers even more than sufficient healthy protein to please the body's demands without all the artery-clogging saturated fats that are present in the current American diet plan.

As a vegan endurance professional athlete, I put a high-stress level on my body. I have to admit my plant-based diet plan has sustained me for years without any adverse effect on structure, lean muscular tissue mass, or recuperation.

# NOT ALL HEALTHY PROTEIN IS DEVELOPED EQUIVALENT

Healthy protein is composed of parts called amino acids. Throughout food digestion, your body will certainly break down the healthy protein right into these amino acids and will utilize them for various processes in your body. A few of these uses consist of constructing bones, muscle mass, and various other body cells, producing hormonal agents, and sustaining natural chemical features.

There are 22 amino acids, 9 of which your body cannot make, so they should be acquired from your diet plan. These are generally called vital amino acids.

Numerous plant-based healthy protein resources have some, yet not every one of the crucial amino acids. This makes it essential to consume a range of these vegetarian or vegan foods throughout the day.

*Here's a list of my top plant-based foods high in protein:*

## Quinoa

A grain-like seed, quinoa is a great healthy protein choice that can be substituted to rice or pasta, offered alone or over greens and vegetables. It can be offered cool with almond or with coconut milk and berries, it provides an excellent base for a veggie burger and is likewise an amazing morning meal grain.

## Tempeh

A fermented soybean-based food, tempeh is a healthy and balanced protein-packed option to its non-fermented relative: tofu. It is an ingredient to a wonderful veggie burger and functions as a yummy meat substitution option to meatballs in pasta, or over wild rice and veggies.

Tempeh contains 31 grams of healthy protein per cup.

Tempeh is made from fermented entire soybeans and supplies vitamin B, iron, and calcium. The nutrients are much better taken in from tempeh than they are from tofu since it is fermented. Tempeh additionally has prebiotic fiber that feeds the excellent microorganisms in our digestive tract, enhancing the intestine health and wellness, and decreasing the swelling in the body.

## Lentils

These beans provide intricate carbs for continual power and well-balanced blood glucose levels. The soluble fiber they have feed excellent germs in the gut fundamental for us because they aid at maintain us healthy and balanced and might reduce cholesterol, overall and LDL (frequently called "negative" cholesterol). Lentils are abundant in iron, as well.

At 18 grams of healthy protein per prepared cup (240 ml), lentils are an excellent resource of healthy protein.

They can be used in a range of recipes, varying from fresh salads to spice-infused dahls and hearty soups.

Lentils additionally have excellent quantities of gradually absorbed carbohydrates, and a single cup (240 ml) supplies about 50% of your suggested everyday fiber consumption.

The kind of fiber found in lentils has been revealed to feed the great microorganisms in your colon, advertising a healthy and balanced digestive tract. Lentils might additionally help in reducing the danger of heart problems, diabetes mellitus, excess body weight, and some kinds of cancer cells.

Additionally, lentils are abundant in manganese, folate, and iron. They additionally include an excellent quantity of antioxidants and various other health-promoting plant substances.

Lentils are dietary giants. They are abundant in healthy protein and consist of great quantities of various other nutrients. They might likewise help in reducing the danger of numerous illnesses.

## Walnuts

Unlike various other nuts, walnuts include a considerable quantity of the omega-3 fat referred to as alpha-linolenic acid (ALA), which aids the heart and the mind. They likewise flaunt extra antioxidant power than various other nuts, assisting to shield the body from totally free extreme damages. Walnuts have been revealed to enhance cognitive features.

## Pumpkin seeds

These yummy seeds have health-promoting omega-3 fats connected with preserving a healthy and balanced heart. You'll obtain a healthy and balanced dosage of fiber, zinc, magnesium, B vitamins, and various other nutrients as well when you consume them. Furthermore, research studies have revealed that consuming pumpkin seeds can assist improve testosterone levels for males.

## Almond butter

Almonds, and almond butter, are abundant resources of minerals (calcium, magnesium, selenium) in addition to folic acid, potassium, vitamin E, and selenium, assisting to cover your dietary bases. According to a research study, almonds might lower LDL (known as "poor") cholesterol and cardiovascular disease risks. They're additionally considered to maintain blood sugar level degrees in check and secure versus colon cancer cells.

## Maca powder

This superfood invigorates without being an energizer and contains significant amounts of vitamin C, calcium, potassium, and magnesium. Maca aids to preserve the balance, and the equilibrium of the body lowers anxiety levels, and it might relieve anxiety and anxiousness.

## Chia seeds

Chia seeds are stemmed from the Salvia hispanica plant, which grows both in Mexico and Guatemala.

At 6 grams of healthy protein and 13 grams of fiber per 1.25 ounces (35 grams), chia seeds certainly deserve their spot on this checklist.

What's even more, these little seeds consist of a great quantity of iron, magnesium, calcium, and selenium, along with omega-3 fats, antioxidants, and numerous other advantageous plant substances.

They're likewise extremely flexible. Chia seeds have this peculiar quality of becoming a gel-like compound if immersed and let to get soaked in water or any other liquid. This makes them a very easy enhancement to a selection of dishes, varying from smoothie mixes to baked products and chia desserts.

Chia seeds are a useful resource of plant healthy protein. They additionally consist of a range of vitamins, minerals, antioxidants, and various other health-promoting substances.

## Flaxseeds

These seeds have the highest degree of omega-3 fat alpha-linolenic acid (ALA) of all plant foods, along with an optimal proportion of omega-3 to omega-6 fats. Flaxseeds aid the equilibrium of estrogen levels, ease menopausal signs and have resulted to boost the prostate-cancer defense. In individuals with coronary artery conditions, they have been located to enhance triglyceride levels and high blood pressure.

## Seitan

A superb replacement for beef, soy, and fish products, one offering offers about 25% of your RDA of healthy protein. Not for those with gluten level of sensitivities, as it is made from wheat gluten.

Seitan is a preferred healthy protein resource for numerous vegetarians and vegans.

It is made from gluten, the primary healthy protein in wheat. Unlike lots of soy-based simulated meats, it has the appearance and the structure of meat when prepared.

Recognized as wheat meat or wheat gluten, it has more or less 25 grams of healthy protein per 3.5 ounces (100 grams). This makes it the wealthiest plant healthy protein resource on this checklist.

Seitan is additionally an excellent resource of selenium and has percentages of iron, phosphorus, and calcium.

You can find this meat choice in the fridges of the majority of organic food shops, or you can make your very own variation with essential wheat gluten utilizing my recipe.

Seitan can be pan-fried, smoked, or even sautéed. It can be conveniently included in a selection of dishes.

Seitan must be avoided by individuals with a gastric condition or gluten level of sensitivity.

Seitan is a kind of simulated meat made from wheat gluten. Its high healthy protein material, meat-like appearance, and adaptability make it a prominent plant-based healthy protein selection amongst lots of vegetarians and vegans.

## Chickpeas and most varieties of beans

Kidney, black, pinto, and most various other selections of beans, include high quantities of healthy protein per offering.

Chickpeas, additionally referred to as garbanzo beans, are one more bean with a high healthy protein net content.

Both chickpeas and beans include a high 15 grams of healthy protein per prepared cup (240 ml). They are additionally an outstanding resource of complex carbohydrates, fiber, iron, folate, phosphorus, potassium, manganese, and numerous helpful plant substances.

Numerous research studies reveal that a diet regimen abundant in beans and various other vegetables can lower cholesterol, aid regulate blood sugar levels, reduced blood stress, and reduce belly fat.

Include beans to your diet plan by making delicious dishes of homemade chili or appreciate additional health and wellness benefits by spraying a dashboard of turmeric extract on baked chickpeas.

Beans are health-promoting, protein-packed that contain a selection of vitamins, minerals, and helpful plant substances. I particularly enjoy eating beans. Great on a veggie burrito, in soups and chili, on salads or over rice with veggies, beans of all ranges are an everyday staple of my diet plan.

## Hempseed

Hempseed originates from the Cannabis sativa plant, which is infamous for coming from the very same family as the cannabis plant.

Hempseed has just trace quantities of THC, the substance that creates the marijuana-like medication results.

Not as widely known as various other seeds, hempseed contains 10 grams of the total, conveniently absorbable healthy protein per ounce (28 grams). That's 50% greater than chia seeds and flaxseeds.

Hempseed likewise has an excellent quantity of magnesium, iron, zinc, calcium, and selenium. What's even more, it is an excellent resource of omega-3 and omega-6 fats in the proportion thought to be optimum for human health and wellness.

Surprisingly, some researches show that the sort of fats located in hempseed might help in reducing swelling, along with reducing signs of PMS, menopause, and particular skin diseases.

You can include hemp seed to your diet regimen by scattering some in your smoothie mix or early morning muesli. It can likewise be utilized in homemade salad dressings or healthy protein bars.

Hempseed consists of an excellent quantity of total, highly-digestible healthy protein, in addition to health-promoting vital fats in a proportion optimum for human health and wellness.

## Nutritional yeast

Nutritional yeast is a shutdown pressure of Saccharomyces cerevisiae yeast, marketed readily as a yellow powder or flakes.

It has a tacky consistency that makes it a prominent active ingredient in meals like mashed potatoes and clambered tofu.

Nutritional yeast can additionally be sprinkled to season pasta dishes or perhaps be enjoyed as a tasty topping on snacks.

This abundant resource of plant healthy protein supplies the body with 14 grams of healthy protein and 7 grams of fiber per ounce (28 grams).

Strengthened dietary yeast is additionally an exceptional resource of zinc, magnesium, copper, manganese, and all the B vitamins, especially B12.

The yeast is unfortified, but you shouldn't really count on dietary yeast as your only source of vitamin B12.

Nutritional yeast is a prominent plant-based active ingredient frequently used to offer meals a dairy-free cheese taste. It is high in healthy protein, fiber and is usually strengthened with numerous nutrients, vitamins, and especially vitamin B12.

## Spelt and teff

Spelt and teff comes from a classification called old grains. Various other old grains consisting of einkorn, farro, sorghum, and barley come from the same group.

Spelt is a sort of wheat and includes gluten, whereas teff stems from a yearly turf, which suggests it is gluten-free.

Spelt and teff give between 10-11 grams of healthy protein per prepared cup (240 ml), making them greater in healthy protein than various other old grains.

Both are outstanding resources of numerous nutrients, consisting of intricate carbohydrates, fiber, iron, manganese, magnesium, and phosphorus. They additionally have excellent quantities of B vitamins, zinc, and selenium.

Spelt and teff are functional choices to substitute your typical grains, such as wheat and rice, and can be used in numerous dishes varying from baked items to polenta and risotto.

Spelt and teff are high-protein old grains. They're an excellent resource of different minerals and vitamins and an intriguing choice to even more usual grains.

## Green peas

The little green peas typically acted as a side recipe consists of 9 grams of healthy protein per prepared cup (240 ml), which is somewhat greater than the content of protein in a cup of milk.

What's even more, an offering of green peas covers greater than 25% of your day-to-day fiber, vitamin A, C, K, folate, manganese, and thiamine demands.

Green peas are additionally an excellent resource of iron, magnesium, phosphorus, zinc, copper, and a number of various other B vitamins.

You can utilize peas in dishes such as pea and basil packed kinds of pasta, Thai-inspired pea soup or pea and avocado guacamole.

Green peas are high in healthy protein, minerals, and vitamins and can be used as greater than simply a side meal.

## Spirulina

This turquoise alga is absolutely a dietary giant.

2 tablespoons (30 ml) give you 8 grams of total healthy protein, along with covering 22% of your everyday demands of iron and thiamin, and 42% of your daily copper requirements.

Spirulina, moreover, has good quantities of magnesium, riboflavin, manganese, potassium, and high percentages of a lot of the various other nutrients your body demands, consisting of crucial fats.

Phycocyanin, an all-natural pigment located in spirulina, shows up to have effective antioxidant, anti-cancer, and anti-inflammatory residential properties

Researches connect taking in spirulina to wellness advantages varying from a more robust immune system, minimized blood stress to improve blood sugar and cholesterol levels.

Spirulina is a nutritious, high-protein food with lots of advantageous health-enhancing buildings.

## Ezekiel bread and various other kinds of bread made from sprouted grains

Ezekiel bread is made from natural, grew whole grains and beans. These breads are made of wheat, millet, barley, and spelt, along with lentils and soybeans.

2 pieces of Ezekiel bread have about 8 grams of healthy protein, which is somewhat greater than the ordinary Bread.

Growing vegetables, and grains, enhances the quantity of healthy and balanced nutrients they consist of and decreases the number of anti-nutrients in them.

On top of that, research studies reveal that rising increases their amino acid material. Lysine is the limiting amino acid in several plants, and rising boosts the lysine net content - this aids in improving the total healthy protein of high quality.

Integrating grains with vegetables can, even more, boost the bread's amino acid account.

Growing additionally appears to enhance the bread's soluble fiber, folate, vitamin C, vitamin E, and beta-carotene net content. It might also decrease somewhat the gluten material, which can boost food digestion in those that are bothered by gluten.

Ezekiel and various other bread made from grown grains have an improved healthy protein and nutrient account, contrasted to even more conventional bread.

## Soy milk

Milk that's made from soybeans and strengthened with minerals, and vitamins, is a wonderful alternative to cow's milk.

It does not it include just 7 grams of healthy protein per cup (240 ml), yet, it is likewise an outstanding resource of calcium, vitamin D and vitamin B12

Keep in mind that soy milk and soybeans do not normally consist of vitamin B12, so choosing a strengthened range is advised.

Soy milk is found in a lot of grocery stores. It is an exceptionally functional product that can be eaten by itself or added to a range of food preparation and cooking recipes.

It is a great suggestion to select bitter ranges to maintain the quantity of sugar to a minimum.

Soy milk is a high-protein plant option to cow's milk. It is a flexible item that can be made use of in a selection of means.

## Oats and oatmeal

Oats are a tasty and very easy food to include in a diet plan, and it is an excellent source of plant-based healthy protein.

Fifty percent of a cup (120 ml) of completely dry oats gives you about 6 grams of healthy protein and 4 grams of fiber. This portion additionally includes great quantities of magnesium, zinc, folate, and phosphorus.

Oats are not taken into consideration a full, healthy protein, but it does include higher-quality healthy protein than various other frequently eaten grains like rice and wheat.

You can make use of oats in a selection of dishes varying from oatmeal to veggie hamburgers. They can be grounded directly into the flour and used for cooking.

Oats are not just nourishing yet additionally a tasty and a very easy method to include plant healthy protein right into a vegan or vegetarian diet regimen.

## Basmati rice

Basmati rice consists of about 1.5 times as much healthy protein as various other long-grain rice selections, consisting of wild rice and basmati.

One prepared cup (240 ml) gives 7 grams of healthy protein, along with a great quantity of fiber, manganese, magnesium, phosphorus, vitamin b, and copper.

Unlike white rice, basmati rice is not removed from its bran. This is excellent from a dietary viewpoint, as bran includes fiber and a lot of minerals and vitamins.

This creates issues concerning arsenic, which can build up in the bran of rice plants expanded in contaminated locations. Arsenic is a poisonous micronutrient that might trigger different illnesses, particularly when consumed consistently for extended periods of time. Cleaning basmati rice before the food preparation and its use is fundamental, so use a lot of water to steam it - this might minimize the arsenic content by as much as 57%.

Basmati rice is a yummy, nutrient-rich plant resource of healthy protein. Those depending on basmati rice as a food staple must take safety measures to decrease its arsenic net content.

## Protein-rich fruits and vegetables

All vegetables, and fruits, include healthy protein, yet the quantities are generally little.

Some have even more than others.

Veggies with one of the healthiest proteins consist of broccoli, spinach, asparagus, artichokes, potatoes, wonderful potatoes, and Brussels sprouts.

They have around 4-5 grams of healthy protein per prepared cup. Practically a grain, pleasant corn is a usual food that has around as much healthy protein as these high-protein veggies

Fresh fruits usually have a reduced healthy protein net content than veggies. Those include guava, cherimoyas, mulberries, bananas, blackberries, and nectarines, which have about 2-4 grams of healthy protein per cup.

Specific vegetables and fruits include even more healthy protein than others. Include them in your dishes to enhance your everyday healthy protein consumption.

## Take-home message

Healthy protein shortages amongst vegans and vegetarians are much too common from being the standard.

Some individuals might be interested in raising their plant healthy protein consumption for a selection of factors.

This listing can be utilized as an overview for any individual curious about integrating a lot more plant-based proteins right into their diet plan.

# CHAPTER 9: WHAT IS PLANT-BASED PROTEIN POWDER?

Plant-based healthy protein powder is a very prominent nutritional resource that includes switching animal-based resources for plant-based foods. Performing on the very same principle of healthy protein powders as a whole, plant-based protein powders take a different method in the direction of presenting various resources for general health and wellness assistance with the common advantages that occur with making use of these detailed sources.

Out of the many wellness advantages, a current 2016 research study at the Academy of Nutrition and Dietetics, verified that individuals that ate even more plant-based nutrients had decreased the risks of persistent health and wellness problems. These problems can be identified as the following conditions:

- Ischemic heart disease.
- Type 2 diabetes.
- Hypertension.
- Cancer.
- Obesity.

These plant-based nutrients have moreover been identified to be better suited for all people, especially for professional athletes, kids, and elders, and have been revealed to be valuable to women that are expecting.

As you can see, there are numerous advantages of plant-based healthy protein. By integrating the useful resources right into a healthy powder kind, you can attain a precise healthy protein usage with every one of the vital qualities of plant-based nutrients.

## What's inside plant-based protein powder?

With the ever-growing demand to incorporate for a total and complete plant-based healthy protein formula, there are several components you might have seen on the back of supplement tags when you see your regional GNC and Vitamin Shoppe.

Numerous significant resources can be developed into total healthy proteins such as:

- Pea protein.
- Sacha Inchi.
- Sunflower seed.
- Pumpkin seed.
- Hemp protein.
- Soy.
- Chia.
- Brown rice protein.
- Yellow pea protein.

## Pea protein

Pea Protein is a high healthy protein resource obtained from yellow peas and consists of all the important amino acids that would certainly originate from a plant-based replacement in which your body cannot normally generate. This resource is reduced in the amount of healthy proteins in contrast to the qualities of what you would certainly locate with a soy isolate. In general, this is an excellent use for an alternative over animal-based healthy protein.

**Sacha Inchi**

Sacha Inchi has shaken the health market demand with the buzz of excitement after it was identified as a large Superfood compared to an elegant plant-based resource. These seeds have a similar aesthetic to a dark baked peanut even though they remain in truth in the seeds group. What makes Sacha Inchi unique is the amazing health and wellness advantages that are connected to this seed, consisting of:

- Weight loss.
- Contain healthy and balanced fats and omegas.
- They are a total healthy protein.
- Links to total joint and bone health and wellness.
- The healthy and balanced omega-3's aid with skin and hair advantages.

**Sunflower seed protein**

The Sunflower Seed really has a large quantity of healthy protein and is most generally used within cooking and food preparation. Sunflower Seed healthy protein likewise has countless wellness advantages, and it is filled with Vitamin E. Several of these advantages contain:

- Anti-inflammation.
- Lowers cholesterol.
- Reduces risk of heart attack.

## Pumpkin sed protein

While the pumpkin seeds' healthy protein could not be the only source of protein as it does not contain all the amino acids, it can be integrated with several resources to offset. Pumpkin seed healthy protein is additionally extremely high in healthy protein net content and can be used as an exceptional resource for nutrients and included advantages. Several of these unique advantages consist of:

- • Antioxidants to reduce inflammation.
- • Reduced risk of certain cancers.
- • Improved urinary tract disorder.

## Hemp protein

Hemp, a strain of the prominent Sativa plant, gets on as documented to be among the fastest expanding plants and has been commonly used as a complete healthy protein resource as it has all the 9 necessary amino acids that the body requires.

## Soy

Soy healthy protein is originated from soybeans that are additionally a total healthy protein resource with rapid health and wellness advantages. According to research on the usage of healthy soy protein over animal-based healthy protein, it was revealed that over some time, its consumption caused the reduction of cholesterol. Soy can be utilized as a single source or can be incorporated with various other plant-based active ingredients for fantastic protein-packed food.

There have been some debates bordering the overuse of soy and intake for men as it enhances general estrogen degrees.

While this has been a small heading in current information, it ought to be well-noted that it has really been revealed by some professionals to be great for other wellness results.

## Chia

Chia seeds are a widely known 'superfood' with fantastic healthy protein net content (relying on the complete quantity) and have been used for quite a long time. Chia seeds are additionally a full, healthy protein and have been proven to be a great enhancement to any plant-based healthy protein formula or matrix.

## Wild rice protein

Commonly considered as among the most effective kinds of healthy protein powder, wild rice might not be taken into consideration as a full, healthy protein, however, it is extra popular to be accosted with a top-level mix of various other plant-based resources for a well-balanced mixture.

## Yellow pea protein

Yellow pea healthy protein is frequently neglected in particular areas, yet, it has been connected to numerous health and wellness benefits and advantages varying from the general heart and kidney wellness.

This is moreover a full, healthy protein which contains all crucial amino acids required.

A few of these could have you assuming, "Wow, this has to taste horrible when blended."

Well, you may be right on this. Several plant-based resources aren't always most likely to taste 'great'. On the other hand, you might have currently attempted a plant-based healthy protein before and could not wait to wash your mouth out with water.

Responding to the dreadful preference for sweeter things and their taste can typically be difficult to mask without filling the concoction up with sweetening agents such as sucralose. Where does this leave the 'All-Natural' technique with plant-based healthy protein powders then?

# CHAPTER 10: PROTEIN INTAKE FOR MUSCLE BUILDING

## Understanding protein intake for muscle building on a plant-based diet

Healthy protein is not just crucial for a healthy and balanced diet plan and a smooth operating body; however, it is likewise a champ at developing and reinforcing muscular tissue mass.

While several individuals are mindful of animal-based resources of healthy protein, there are really a host of unbelievably varied, healthy and balanced, and effective all-natural plant-based resources. Plant-based proteins are not only merely as efficient as animal resources of healthy protein, they additionally provide the body with vitamins, minerals, and various other abundant nutrients (such as antioxidants, flavonoids, and polyphenols).

Keeping that claimed, even if you recognize where you pick to gather your healthy protein, just how much suffices? Just how much is way too much? Is there an appropriate proportion to optimize your muscular tissue enhancing ventures?

The response is, of course, to all! To aid you in discovering your ideal protein-muscle proportion, continue reading and get all the information you need!

# WHY IS PROTEIN ESSENTIAL FOR MUSCLES

Healthy protein is one of the 3 macronutrients - materials that "give calories for power" - that are necessary for your body: carbs, fat, and healthy protein. When it comes to healthy protein, every gram provides up to 4 calories, and 15 percent of your weight is made of up of these grams of healthy protein.

What is healthy protein best at? It is best to create the structure of muscular tissue mass. Healthy proteins are real "structure blocks of muscular tissue mass," implying you cannot construct solid muscular tissues without sufficient resources of healthy and balanced protein.

# EXACTLY HOW DOES IT FUNCTION?

It does not just fix, it additionally loads in the injury and making it "larger and more powerful," and as a result, developing even more muscular tissue mass. If your body does not have sufficient healthy protein to fix the splits, your body cannot construct more muscular tissue mass.

# LEARNING MORE ABOUT YOUR COMPLETE PROTEINS

While any plant-based food that is abundant in healthy protein benefits your muscle mass, there is a group described as "full healthy proteins" or "optimal healthy proteins" that are incredibly proficient at developing muscular tissue.

The term total healthy protein describes a healthy protein which contains all the 9 crucial amino acids - these are amino acids that cannot be created by the body, yet they should be just eaten using the food you consume. The 9 crucial amino acids consist of "histidine, isoleucine, leucine, lysine, methionine, phenylalanine, tryptophan, valine and threonine." Ideal or total healthy proteins are sometimes additionally described as top-quality healthy proteins because it is what they are... well... they are of extremely premium quality.

Plant-based resources of full, healthy proteins consist of vegan-friendly staples such as quinoa, chia seeds, soy, and hemp seeds.

Hemp healthy protein - that "comes from the hemp plant, which does not have THC (the energetic component in cannabis)" - is vegan-friendly, easily offered at your neighborhood grocery store, and is packed complete of lean, healthy protein. One cup of raw soybeans contains an amount of 67 grams of healthy protein, while a cup of steamed soybeans provides 28 grams of healthy protein.

## Best protein-rich plant-based foods for muscle strengthening

Per the USDA, it is essential to comply with 2 standards when picking healthy proteins for a well-balanced, healthy and well-adjusted, muscle mass structure diet plan: pick leaner and extra diverse, healthy proteins. The checklist of plant-based healthy protein choices is long, varied, and vivid.

*Below are several of the leading protein-rich resources:*

- Navy Beans (20 grams per cup).
- Chickpeas (7.25 grams per 1/2 cup).
- Lentils (13 grams per cup).
- Peanut Butter (8 grams per tbsp).
- Almonds (16.5 grams per 1/2 cup).
- Quinoa (8 grams per 1-cup offering).
- Edamame (8 grams per half-cup offering).
- Soba Noodles (12 grams per 3-ounce offering).
- Spirulina (8 grams per 2 tbsps).
- Chia Seeds (2 grams per tbsp).
- Hemp Seeds (5 grams per tbsp).
- Potatoes (8 grams per offering).
- Tofu (10 grams per 1/2 cup for company tofu).
- Tempeh (15 grams per 1/2 cup).
- Seitan (21 grams per 1/3 cup).

You might observe that there aren't that many vegetables on the checklist. While some veggies do contain some percentages of healthy protein - such as kale, mushrooms, and broccoli - they do not supply sufficient healthy protein to sustain a bodybuilding diet plan alone. Keeping that stated, set your preferred vegetable with among the above protein-rich choices, and you are not just offering your body adequate healthy protein yet various other crucial nutrients and minerals.

# RECOGNIZING THE PROTEIN TO MUSCLE RATIO

You'll listen to some clashing information when it comes to healthy protein intake versus muscular tissue conditioning or structure muscular tissue mass. This results from the truth that several aspects play into just how promptly or gradually each private body will certainly accumulate muscle mass. Age, sex, exercise levels, kind of exercise, selection of exercise, sources of healthy protein, the quantity of healthy protein, and when you are taking in healthy protein are just a few of these variables.

Without employing a costly individual fitness instructor or nutritional expert, how do you individuate the ideal equilibrium of healthy protein to the physical task to personal private variables?

# DISCOVERING YOUR PERFECT PROTEIN RATIO

Seeking advice from a specialist is a great idea. A few of us do not have the opportunity for numerous factors. All you require to recognize are a couple of straightforward standards that you can use to your circumstance, in brief, the healthy protein to bodyweight proportion!

Whether you are looking to gain muscular tissue mass, or merely straighten yourself, you will increase your healthy protein consumption, as it logically suggests much more muscle tissue.

*This is not the case*

Consuming over the advised quantity of healthy protein might be dangerous. For the ordinary adult, day-to-day healthy protein intake is around "0.37 grams per extra pound of body weight, and that amounts to about 56 grams of complete healthy protein for a 150-pound grownup."

When you have reached your objective using the 10 to 35 percent criteria, you can, after that, eat healthy protein in a modest and regular method utilizing the 0.37 grams per extra pound of body-weight standard.

# CHAPTER 11: NATURAL PROTEIN SUPPLEMENTS FOR VEGETARIANS & VEGANS

Obtaining ample healthy protein from entire vegan foods alone can be challenging; this is where taking a healthy protein supplement comes in. Some of the vegan, and vegetarian healthy protein supplements, consist of:

## Whey healthy protein

Whey healthy protein is a supplement referred to as an efficiently-used healthy protein. It originates from milk, and it is generally used for post-workout healing. Study reveals that it can additionally enhance cognitive features, specifically in grownups with high tiredness.

## Pea healthy protein

This is a wonderful hypoallergenic alternative, without milk, grains, soy, and egg. Pea healthy protein is well-tolerated, so it can be worth a shot if you usually have a tough time absorbing healthy protein.

## Rice healthy protein

Rice healthy protein is relatively neutral in taste, making it very easy to have it on-the-go or mix it into healthy smoothies. This is likewise a terrific choice for those on a vegan diet plan.

## Chia seed healthy protein

These little seeds ring contains about 6 grams of healthy protein per 1/4 cup, and are progressively utilized in healthy protein powders. Chia healthy protein is typically grown, a procedure that includes the saturation of the seed, which can assist with food digestion.

## Soy healthy protein

You can utilize it as one more gluten-free and a dairy-free choice if you think soy is best for you should include it in your diet plan. Some individuals have found out that soy has a somewhat nutty aftertaste.

There are several choices to maintain healthy protein levels high while getting on a vegan or a vegetarian diet plan. Alternatives, and substitutes, are readily available to make sure you get a sufficient healthy protein intake every day. As usual, we advise contacting your specialist to see if a brand-new supplement is right for your therapy strategy.

# CHAPTER 12: MACRONUTRIENTS

"Will it certainly fit my macros" is a usual statement in the dish preparation and a healthy and balanced way of life room. The attitude is, "I understand specifically what you must be consuming (based upon my customized macronutrient numbers) to shed fat, placed on my muscle mass, or keep weight, after that, it does not matter if you consume pizza, brownies, cookies, or a salad". Is that truly the instance?

You have most likely listened to many talks about macros if you have been in the health and fitness environment for any length of time. Comprehending the truths behind macros and concerning your individual dietary needs will certainly make a difference in your very own wellness journey. In this chapter, we'll discover what macros are, exactly how to recognize if you are consuming the appropriate proportions and the very best foods for supplying them.

# WHAT ARE MACRONUTRIENTS?

Macronutrients are the food classifications that give you the power to bring out our fundamental human features, and they are boiled down right into 3 groups; healthy protein, fats, and carbs. When you recognize precisely how to determine your macros, it is simple to figure out just how much calories you are placing in your body every day and just how much energy you require to burn off the extra calories.

The 3 macronutrients are carbs, fats, and healthy proteins, and they all have various duties in your body. Generally, you'll drop weight. If you desire to obtain an insight into how to monitor your macros, then keep reading.

*Carbohydrates:*

Composed of starches and sugars, carbohydrates are the macronutrient that your system most calls for. Your body breaks down a lot of carbs as soon as they are ingested, so they are accountable for providing you with an essential source of energy. Unless you get on a specialized consuming strategy like the ketogenic diet plan, carbohydrates ought to compose roughly 45-65% of your caloric requirements.

Carbs provide your body with sugar, its key energy source. When sugar goes into a cell, a collection of metabolic responses transforms it right into ATP (Adenosine Tri-Phosphate), which is a kind of temporary power. Any extra sugar is changed right into a starch called glycogen, which is saved in the liver and as body fat for later usage.

Not all carbs are developed equivalent, as not all carbs are quickly absorbable or can be used for power manufacturing. Cellulose, as an example, is a non-digestible carb found in vegetables and fruits that serves as a nutritional fiber. This indicates that it aids the body get rid of waste from the big intestinal tract, subsequently maintaining it in functioning order.

Much shorter particles are much easier for your body to break down, so they are identified as basic. Complicated carbohydrates, in comparison, are bigger particles that your body takes longer to break down. In spite of these distinctions, a carbohydrate is a carbohydrate in concerns to your macros.

*Healthy protein:*

All healthy proteins are made up of mixes of twenty various amino acids, which your body subsequently damages apart and incorporates to develop various physical structures. In other words, your body requires healthy protein to sustain the body's organ performance, power enzyme responses, and to construct your hair, nails, and various other cells.

Of the twenty amino acids, 9 are categorized as necessary, implying that your body cannot produce them, so you require to take them in via food. Those that consume a plant-based diet regimen rather than following an omnivorous diet can likewise satisfy their amino acid requirements by consuming a healthy diet plan that is composed of numerous plant-based resources of healthy protein like nuts, vegetables, and entire grains.

Like carbs, one gram of healthy protein includes 4 calories.

*Fat:*

In spite of their destructive credibility in previous years, you should not outlaw fats from your diet plan. Your body requires fats to remain healthy and balanced, and in between 10-35% of your food needs to be composed of this macronutrient.

Fats additionally work as a power source, as it is your body's recommended approach for saving extra calories. Your system will just keep percentages of sugar in your cells, yet body fat allows you safe and secure unrestricted amounts of power rather, which you use while resting, throughout the workout, and in between meals.

When you start consuming fats, you are required to guarantee that you provide your system with fats it needs, and that cannot make itself, like omega-3 and omega-6 fats. You can find omega-3s in oily fish, eggs and walnuts, and omega-6s from a lot of veggie oils.

Nutritional fat assists your body to soak up fat-soluble vitamins like A, D, E, and K, and it adds taste and structure to your food. There are 3 main sorts of nutritional fat (hydrogenated fat, unsaturated fat, and trans-fat), and they all have various influences on your wellness.

**Hydrogenated fat:** found in meat, butter, lotion, and various other animal resources.
**Unsaturated fat:** found in olive oil, nuts, avocados, canola oil, and various other plant resources.
**Trans fats:** found in industrial items like junk food, convenience food, and margarine.

It is crucial to keep in mind that you ought to decrease your trans fats intake as much as possible. Frequently called "Franken fats," trans fats can enhance your risks of coronary cardiovascular disease and weight problems.

# WATER

Water makes up a considerable part of our bodies. It manages our body temperature level and helps in the metabolic process.

The Institute of Medicine suggests drinking 13 cups of water (more or less 3 liters) for males and 9 cups (or 2.2 liters) for females. Not sure if you are getting enough water?

# SHOULD YOU COUNT MACRONUTRIENTS INSTEAD OF CALORIES?

Thinking that calories are the typical means to evaluate your food consumption, why would you take into consideration switching over to grams of macronutrients? The main factor that calories aren't excellent for determining just how healthy and balanced your food options are is that they do not take into consideration what you are consuming. 100 calories of broccoli will certainly rate the exact same as 100 calories of cake, though the 2 could not be more different from a nutritional standpoint.

Changing over to counting your macros, on the other hand, takes top quality food and satiation right into account. By tracking your macro needs, you have a much better possibility of complying with a diet plan that makes good sense for your health and wellness.

# JUST HOW TO FIGURE OUT YOUR MACRONUTRIENT REQUIREMENTS

While nutritional experts advise particular proportions of each macronutrient for ideal health and wellness, every person's dietary demands will certainly be various. You can identify your specific macronutrient levels with these actions.

*1. Identify your calorie requirements*

Your day-to-day calorie requirements depend on lots of variables, including your age, weight, physical fitness level, and a lot more. You can establish your degrees by tracking what you consume in an ordinary week (one in which you aren't shedding or getting weight). The ordinary degree from nowadays is an excellent indication of your calorie requirements.

*2. Transform calorie counts to macronutrients*

You can designate these calories in the direction of macronutrients based on the proportion you are following when you understand your calorie targets. Frequently, the macronutrient intakes varies between (AMDR) 45-65% of your day-to-day calories from carbohydrates, 20-35% from fats, and 10-35% from healthy protein.

Next off, you can identify the variety of grams to you readily available with standard mathematics. Right here's an instance:

By thinking you require 2,000 calories daily, you can establish your fat consumption by increasing 2,000 by 0.20 (the proportion of fat for 40:40:20 macronutrient divides). That completes 400, which is the variety of daily calories to dedicate to nutritional fat. To establish your gram consumption, divide 400 by 9 (the calories in a gram of fat) for a complete need of 44 grams of fat daily.

# TIPS FOR TRACKING YOUR MACRONUTRIENTS

Are you prepared to begin checking your macro levels? One vital action is identifying which foods will certainly aid you to achieve your goals. Eat your carbohydrates, healthy protein, and fat, so if you stick to eating those, you will make sure you are optimizing your macros.

Stick to top-quality plant-based foods as long as feasible to guarantee you obtain ample quantities of essential elements like minerals and vitamins. A few of the very best foods for consuming for macros consist of the following:

**Fat**: almonds, coconut oil, grass-fed butter, avocados, olive oil, and macadamia nuts.
**Healthy protein**: eggs, nuts, quinoa, and beans.
**Carbohydrates**: leafy environment-friendlies, entire grains, origin veggies.

Obtain all 3 macros in with every dish to guarantee you do not experience insulin spikes, energy crashes, or food cravings later on.

When you initially begin checking macros, it is ideal to utilize a food range to distribute the grams amount. After you are comfortable eyeballing the quantities, you can place the food straight on your plate.

Following your body's macronutrient requirements is a clever method to remain in control of your health and wellness. The procedure of tracking grams of food could appear challenging, yet with this method, you'll acquire the abilities needed to make sure each dish is healthy enough to enhance your health and wellness.

## Why do individuals count macros?

While we might be used to counting calories, a macro-focused diet plan isn't about the number of calories in your food, instead what sort of calories they are.

"To be healthy and balanced, it is crucial to obtain the best equilibrium of macros in your diet regimen," Dr. Ali states. "Sometimes individuals likewise count macros if they're attempting to drop weight, or for various other factors, such as if they're attempting to ensure they obtain the correct amount of healthy protein they require to get muscular tissue".

Locating that equilibrium suggests recognizing specifically what your body demands and what you intend to acquire or shed. It needs some computations; however, the advantages can be significant.

If It Fits Your Macros (IIFYM) diet regimen merely implies making use of a macro calculator to maintain track of the percent of healthy protein, fats, and the carbohydrates you are consuming.

# IS THERE A FUNDAMENTAL MACRO CALCULATOR ANYBODY CAN UTILIZE?

Yes ... yet it will undoubtedly need some mathematics.

You require to figure out your basal metabolic rate or BMR. This is the rate at which your body utilizes the energy consumed and differs from one person to another. There are on the internet calculators to aid you with this, or you can do the formula on your own.

*For females aged 18-30 it is: 0.0546 x (weight in kilos) + 2.33*
*For those aged 30-60 it is: 0.0407 x (weight in kilos) + 2.90*

You can, after that, use your overall energy expense for a day. If you are much less energetic than the basic population you increase it by 1.49 if you are at an ordinary level, you increase it by 1.63, and if you are much more energetic you increase it by 1.78

*That's the amount of calories you require each day. Still with me?*

From here, you can determine your macro beginning factor. Dr Ali describes: "As a wide estimation, healthy proteins, and carbs, offer us 4 calories for each gram, and fat offers us 9 grams. If you consume a tiny smoked chicken breast, which has 6.4 g of fat and 29g of healthy protein, it would undoubtedly have 58 calories from fat and 116 calories from healthy protein - so 174 calories overall".

"We require around 50% of our calories from carbs, 15% from healthy protein, and 35% from fat, nevertheless, this obviously changes for different people".

"Regardless of whether you are attempting to slim down or construct muscular tissue, you maintain the percentages of 50% carbohydrates, 15% healthy protein, and 35% fat. You would undoubtedly transform the number of calories you would certainly have".

"If you are attempting to slim down, you require 600 calories less than your overall power expense. By doing this, you'll instantly obtain the additional healthy protein and carbohydrate you require to construct muscle mass, yet the percentages continue to be in place".

Applications such as "My Fitness Pal" which has macronutrient rankings and "Fitocracy Macros" are complimentary and can aid you to reach holds with your body's demands and count your macros.

The rationale of the macro diet regimen is that you attempt various dimensions and readjust up until you discover something that matches your needs. The diet plan does not take into account alcohol.

"A glass of rosé can have around 140 calories in it - that's more than a two-finger Ki".

# MACRONUTRIENT PROPORTIONS

Now that we've responded to "What are macronutrients?" we need to highlight that like diet plans and health and fitness, macronutrient proportions are not one-size-fits-all. There is no excellent macronutrient proportion that matches every person, and your demands will certainly alter according to various elements in your life.

An additional factor as to why we do not advise a really detailed macronutrient proportion is that it does not state anything regarding the high quality of the nutrients. A proportion takes into account the variety of macronutrients, which implies that carbohydrates from white sugar and quinoa are assimilated similarly.

*The very best you can do is:*

- Focus on equilibrium.
- Focus on whole foods.
- Enjoy your portion sizes.

Attempting to reach various macronutrient targets permits you to figure out which levels function best for you. These arrays can differ, relying on which kind of diet regimen you are adhering to. Right here are some instances of macro varieties:

## Conventional diet regimen macros array:

- Healthy protein: 10-35% of calories.
- Carbohydrates: 45-65% of calories.
- Fat: 20-35% of calories.

## Low-carb diet plan macros variety:

- Healthy protein: 20-30% of calories.
- Carbohydrates: 30-40% of calories.
- Fat: 30-40% of calories.

# HOW TO CALCULATE MACROS AND TRACK THEM

Time to place our geek cap on! A calorie is a device utilized to determine the energy-producing worth of food, however, this is not one of the most precise procedures. To get a technical explanation, a calorie is specified as the quantity of warmth needed to raise the temperature of one gram of water for one level centigrade.

Each macronutrient has a various calorie degree per gram weight.

- Carb = 4 calories per gram.
- Healthy protein = 4 calories per gram.
- Fat = 9 calories per gram.

The overall calorie net content of food depends on the quantity of carb, healthy protein, and the fat it includes. The thinking was based on the idea that if you get rid of the greater calorie per gram macronutrient, it would certainly be less complicated to minimize the quantity of food.

# CHAPTER 13: PLANT-BASED PROTEIN FILLED DIET AND RECIPES

There's a lengthy listing of veggies that contain sufficient quantities of healthy protein, though just a handful are "complete," suggesting that they include all the 9 of the essential amino acids discovered in healthy animal proteins. If you consume a healthy, vegetable-centric diet plan, you can definitely take pleasure in dishes that contain a high level of healthy protein.

The plant-based diet plan is very easy to follow as it is centered around foods originated from plant resources. Plant-based diet plans applaud on the consummation of fruits, veggies, whole grains, nuts, seeds, and vegetables, suggesting these foods should be the majority of what you consume. To provide you some pointers, our icy veggies are a basic yet tasty place to begin if you are aiming to gradually include even more plants into your lifestyle without making the complete transition in one go.

It is not just a plant-based diet regimen, it is a lot more adaptable and does not boycott milk, meat, fish and shellfish, and eggs completely. And what's even more, flexitarian diet plans advertise eating a vast selection of plant foods, so there are in a program to be adopted in many dietary plans as it gives many advantages.

As a country, we presently have a hard time staying up to date with this number of different diets, nonetheless, with a plant-based diet plan greatly relying upon vegetables and fruit, you are most likely to find it less complicated to eat the advised quantity of food and protein. As smoothies and beans are considerably energizing, you are expected to have a boosted consumption of fiber, vitamins, and minerals – this is very good as many of us are not eating enough fiber! To give you an idea of just how well veggies house a range of dietary advantages, peas offer healthy protein, fiber, folic acid, and vitamin C. It is all-natural to assume that a plant-based diet regimen can bring about an absence of healthy protein, yet this is far from the truth - plants give lots of healthy protein!

If you are attempting to move in the direction of an even more plant-based diet plan, I would suggest you try to get innovative and try out brand-new flavors and mixes that you have never attempted before!

These foods can aid you to satisfy your healthy protein require-ments while supplying lots of taste, macronutrients, and various other nutrients required for a healthy and balanced diet regimen.

Plant-based consuming can imply a lot of changes in your life. Generally speaking, plant-based foods are those that focus on - you thought it - plants, and are reduced in animal-derived products such as meat, dairy products, fowl, fish, and eggs.

Deciding to alter your consuming practices is an individual choice, and one just you can make. Whether you are vegetarian, vegan, or a meat fan, upping your consumption of plant-based foods is a healthy and balanced option. Plant-based diet regimens are connected to a reduced threat of weight problems, cardiovascular disease, kind 2 diabetes mellitus, Alzheimer's, and some cancers cells.

# (7 DAYS) PLANT-BASED MEAL PLAN

Whether you are reducing out meat for health and wellness factors, animal well-being, ecological factors, or if you simply desire to switch over up your recipes, we've designed the best plant-based dish strategy to get you started on your journey.

The dishes we recommend eliminate animal produce and give you to a range of good plant healthy proteins, like tofu, tempeh, entire grains, nuts, and smoothies. This 7-day strategy is ideal for newbies, however, it can be a great addition to vegans and vegetarians.

## Day 1

### Morning meal: Blackberry-citrus granola bowl

Soak the oats overnight for a softer bite. The crispy Coconut-Buckwheat Granola is one of the best comparisons to the velvety consistency of the oats. For your milk of option - I particularly like coconut, almond, or soy milk, but any other kind is good.

*Active ingredients:*

- 2 cups of 2% reduced-fat milk or plain, bitter almond milk or soy milk.
- 1 cup of raw steel-cut oats.
- 1 tbsp of chocolate nibs.
- 1 tbsp of pure syrup.
- 1 cup of coconut-buckwheat granola.
- 1 cup of blackberries.
- 1 cup of slices a red grapefruit and an orange.

*How to make it:*

Combine the milk and the oats in an impermeable container and seal it. Cool it for 8 hrs or overnight for best results.

Add the chocolate chips and the syrup to the oat blend. Separate the oat mix uniformly amongst 4 bowls; topping homogeneously with granola, blackberries, and citrus slices.

*Nutritional values:*

Calories: 403 | Fat: 14.7g | Sat. fat: 5 g | Mono fat: 5.2 g | Poly fat: 3.3 g | Protein: 14 g | Carbohydrate: 57 g | Fiber: 9 g | Cholesterol: 10 mg | Iron: 3 mg | Sodium: 181 mg | Calcium: 190 mg | Sugars: 18 g | Est. sugarcoated: 5g

## Lunch: Sweet potato medallions with almond sauce and chickpea salad

Your 5 active ingredients are far from a high-protein sources, however, they are a significant contribution to this plant-based recipe. The velvety of the almond butter sauce provides lots of taste, while the softness of the potatoes and the chickpeas helps stabilizing the sharp taste of the arugula.

*Active ingredients:*

- 4 little (4-oz.) boiled potatoes.
- 1/4 cup soft all-natural almond butter.
- 3 1/2 tbsp of warm water.
- 3 tbsp of fresh lemon juice, separated.
- 2 tbsp of olive oil, split.
- 1 (15-oz.) can of saltless chickpeas, rinsed and drained properly.
- 5 ounces of baby arugula leaves.
- 3/4 tsp of kosher salt.
- 1 tsp of black pepper.

*How to make it:*

Puncture the potatoes around with a fork; put them on a microwave-safe plate, and then in the microwave at a HIGH voltage until they are tender to the touch (like a boiled potato), This process should take about 5 minutes. Cut them into pieces of a thickness of about ½ inch.

Blend and mash the chickpeas with almond butter, water, and 1 tbsp of lemon juice in a dish - Reserve for later.

Brush potato pieces on 1 side with 1 tbsp oil. Warm up a big frying pan over medium-high heat. Operating in sets, cook the potato pieces, oil side down, till they get gold brownish on the sides, it will take about 2 to 3 mins.

Incorporate the chickpeas, the arugula, salt, pepper, and the 2 tbsps of juice, plus 1 tbsp of oil in a big dish. Split the chickpea blend to 4 plates and cover them with the tasty potato pieces. Drizzle with some almond butter sauce.

*Nutritional values:*

Calories: 379 | Fat: 17 g | Sat. fat: 2.1g | Mono. fat: 10.6 g | Poly fat 2.9 g | Protein: 12 g | Carbohydrate: 47 g | Fiber: 10 g | Cholesterol: 0.0 mg | Iron: 3 mg | Sodium: 493 mg | Calcium: 208 mg | Sugars 7 g | Est. sugarcoated: 1 g

## Supper: Churrasco-style tofu steaks with hemp chimichurri

I suggest you eat this chimichurri filled with parsley cilantro and hemp seeds by the dose that I recommend in this recipe. I guarantee you that it is far better over the classic tofu. The smoky, spice rub and the deep grill marks give a noticeably impressive taste.

*Components:*

- 1 cup of fresh flat-leaf parsley leaves.
- 1 cup of fresh cilantro leaves.
- 2 tbsp of hemp seeds.
- 1 tbsp of merlot vinegar.
- 1 tbsp of fresh lime juice.
- 1 garlic clove.
- 1/4 tsp of smashed red pepper.
- 1 tsp of kosher salt.
- 5 tbsp of extra-virgin olive oil.
- 2 (14-oz.) pkg. of extra-firm block-style tofu carefully drained.
- 2 tsp of garlic powder.
- 1 tsp of onion powder.
- 1 tsp of smoked paprika.
- 1 tsp of ground cumin.
- 1/2 tsp of black pepper cooking spray.

*How to make it*:

*Action 1*

Preheat the stove to 400 ° F. Combine the parsley, the cilantro, the hemp seeds, the vinegar, lime the juice, the garlic, the red pepper, the 1/2 tsp of salt, and the 1/4 cup of oil in a mixer; blend them together till you get a smooth concoction. Reserve for later.

Press the tofu with paper towels up until it is completely dry. First, cut it into halves and then cut the pieces obtained by into thirds. In this way, you should have 12 triangular shapes equal in size.

Incorporate the garlic powder, the onion powder, the smoked paprika, cumin, black pepper, and the rest of 1/2 tsp of salt in a dish. Mix the spices equally on each side of tofu steaks to get an even coat. Spray the pieces with oil.

Warm up 1 tbsp of oil in a grill frying pan over medium-high heat. Lay the tofu steaks in single-layer and let them cook till deep char marks show up, it will take about 3 to 5 mins on each side. Transfer to a flat tray.

Bake the tofu steaks at 400 ° F for 5 mins. Place the 2 tofu steaks on some places, and you should get enough for six people. Top each dish with about 1 tbsp of a natural herb combination.

*Nutritional values:*

Calories: 278 | Fat: 21 g | Sat. fat: 3.3 g | Mono fat: 10.8 g | Poly fat: 6.8 g | Protein: 14 g | Carbohydrate: 8g | Fiber: 1 g | Cholesterol: 0.0 mg | Iron: 3 mg | Sodium 329 mg | Calcium: 119 mg | Sugars: 0 g

# Day 2

## Morning meal: "Huevos" soy-cheros

This recipe is for all those that are looking forward to a plant-based alternative to their preferred animal healthy proteins, like eggs, chorizo, and cheese. This riff on huevos rancheros used turmeric-stained tofu, soy chorizo, and protein-packed pinto beans for a filling up morning meal.

*Active ingredients:*

- 10 ounces of extra-firm block-style tofu, drained.
- 1 tsp of ground turmeric extract.
- 1 tsp of garlic powder.
- 1/2 tsp of chili powder.
- 1/4 tsp of kosher salt.
- 2 tbsp of water.
- 2 tsp of olive oil.
- 1 cup of cut red bell pepper.
- 1 cup of cut green bell pepper.
- 5 ounces of soy chorizo, diced or crumbled (about 3/4 cup).
- 1 (14.5-oz.) can fire-roasted diced tomatoes, undrained.
- 1 cup of drained and washed tinned saltless pinto beans.
- 10 (6-in.) corn tortillas.
- 2 tbsp of lime juice (from 1 lime).
- 1 ripe avocado, cut.
- 1/4 cup of cilantro leaves.

*Exactly how to make it:*

Press the tofu with paper towels up until it is completely dry. Place it on a cutting board and with a fork, reduce it in pieces. Put it aside for later.

Incorporate turmeric extract, garlic powder, chili powder, and salt in a dish. Mix in 2 tbsps of water and put the concoction aside with the tofu.

Add bell peppers to a pan and cook for 5 mins till they are softened. The rest should take about 2 minutes to make: add turmeric mix to the tofu, and mix to uniformly. Cook it for 5 mins or up until the tofu is gently browned.

Warm a different frying pan over medium-high heat. Add the soy chorizo; cook for 3 to 4 mins or till it is browned. Mix in the beans and the tomatoes and cook it for 2 mins or up until everything is heated up.

Prepare 1 tortilla at a time, warm it over medium-high heat straight on the eye of a heater till heated up and charred, for about 15 secs per side.

Place 2 tortillas on each of the 5 plates. Top each with 2/3 cup chorizo blend and 1/2 cup of the tofu blend.

*Nutritional values:*

Calories: 353 | Fat: 15 g | Sat. fat: 1.8 g | Mono fat: 7.2 g | Poly fat 3.7 g | Protein: 15 g | Carbohydrate: 43 g | Fiber: 10 g | Cholesterol: 0.0 mg | Iron: 4 mg | Sodium: 591 mg | Calcium: 169 mg | Sugars: 5 g

## Lunch: Summer salad with tempeh croutons and beet dressing.

Super crispy tempeh creates a remarkable choice for the usual croutons. Throw in a combination of fresh tomatoes, radishes, kale, arugula, and asparagus for a super-filling salad. The combination of tahini and beetroots creates an out-of-the-box food you'll desire over and over.

## Supper: Chickpea and kale curry

Quinoa, peanut butter, and chickpeas integrated into the best plant-powered dish. Mix tasty coconut milk with Indian-inspired spices for a nutty, luscious, and super-filling vegan dish.

*Components:*

- 2 tsp of olive oil.
- 1/2 cup of sliced red bell pepper.
- 1/3 cup of sliced yellow onion.
- 3 cups of cut lacinato kale.
- 2 tsp of diced garlic.
- 1 tsp of curry powder.
- 1/2 tsp of ground ginger.
- 1/2 tsp of kosher salt.
- 1/4 tsp of black pepper.
- 1 tbsp smooth all-natural peanut butter.
- 1 1/2 cups of unsweetened cooled coconut milk (such as Silk).
- 1 cup of tinned saltless chickpeas, rinsed and drained.
- 1 tbsp of fresh lime juice.
- 1 cup of prepared quinoa.
- 2 tbsp of cilantro sprigs.

*How to make it:*

Mix the bell peppers with the onion; cook and stir occasionally until they are softened, it should take about 5 mins. Add the kale and garlic; cook, mixing frequently, up until the kale is softened for about 2 mins. Mix in the coconut milk and the chickpeas, and cook, mixing sometimes, up until the sauce starts to simmer, it should take about 12 to 14 mins.

Place 1/2 cup of prepared quinoa in a dish. Cover it with 1 cup curry mix and cilantro sprigs. You can cool or even freeze the quinoa if you intend to eat it at a later moment.

*Nutritional values:*

Calories: 409 | Fat: 15 g | Sat. fat: 5 g | Uns. fat: 9 g | Protein: 15 g | Carbohydrates: 53 g | Fiber: 11 g | Sugars: 6 g | Added sugars: 0 g | Sodium: 595 mg | Calcium: 48% DV | Potassium: 20% DV

## Day 3

### Morning meal: Peanut butter oats with raspberries

Peanut butter, or indeed any type of nut butter, coupled with nut milk and whole grain creates a protein-dense, delicious way to start your day. The dates add an all-natural sweet taste to the dish - with no added sugars.

We utilize dates to sweeten this morning meal dish - so there are no added refined sugars. For the very best outcomes, select entire dates (pre-chopped dates are usually covered in sugar to prevent them from sticking to each other). Any type of nut butter can be used, and it will certainly have a comparable calorie quality as peanut butter.

*Components:*

- 2 entire dates, sliced.
- 1/2 cup of water.
- 1/2 cup of bitter almond milk.
- 1/2 cup of antique oats.
- 1/8 tsp. of kosher salt.
- 1 Tbsp. of peanut butter (or various other nut butter).
- 1/2 cup of icy or fresh raspberries.

*Exactly how to make it:*

Slowly add water, mashing the dates with a fork to break them up. Include almond milk and bring to a boil. Remove from the heat and mix in the peanut butter.

*Nutritional values:*

Calories: 336 | Fat: 13 g (rested 2 g, unsat 10 g) | Protein: 11 g | Carb: 49 g | Fiber: 10 g | Sugars: 14 g (sugarcoated 0 g) | Sodium: 412 mg | Calc: 31% DV | Potassium: 16% DV

## Lunch: Tempeh gyros with tzatziki

Silken tofu is the secret active ingredient that produces a velvety, yet entirely vegan tzatziki sauce. Allow the tempeh cook down in the tasty sauce pointed out in this recipe, and you'll end up with a delicious alternative.

*Active ingredients:*

- 1 (8-oz.) pkg. of tempeh.
- 1 tbsp of olive oil.
- 1/2 cup of water.
- 1/4 cup of diced yellow onion.
- 2 tbsp of reduced-sodium soy sauce or tamari.
- 1 tsp cut of fresh rosemary.
- 1 tsp of sliced fresh oregano.
- 4 garlic cloves, diced and split.
- 1/4 tsp of black pepper, grounded.
- 3/4 cup of silken tofu (about 6 oz.).
- 1/2 cup of peeled off and grated English cucumber.
- 1 tbsp of fresh lemon juice.
- 1 tbsp of cut fresh dill.
- 1/2 tsp of gewürztraminer vinegar.

- 1/4 tsp of kosher salt.
- 4 (1.9-oz.) whole-grain of flatbread covers (such as flatout flatbread light original).
- 1/2 cup of cut red onion.
- 1 medium tomato, very finely cut.

*How to make it:*

Cut the tempeh lengthwise right into 8 (1/4-inch-thick) pieces.

Pour warm oil in a huge nonstick frying pan and put on the stove. Place the tempeh pieces in the frying pan, and cook till they are golden-brown, for about 3 to 4 mins on each side.

Mix with each other 1/2 cup of water, the diced onion, soy sauce, rosemary, oregano, 2 minced garlic cloves, and 1/8 tsp black pepper in a tiny dish.

Add the soy sauce combination to tempeh in the frying pan. Cover, and reduce the heat to medium-low. Braise the tempeh, turning it sometimes, till the fluid has vaporized and the tempeh has taken in the tastes; it should take about 10 mins.

Refine the silken tofu and the goldened 2 garlic cloves in a high-powered mixer till they are smooth. Place in a dish. Mix in the cucumber, some lemon juice, dill, vinegar, salt, and 1/8 tsp of black pepper.

Separate the tempeh equally amongst the flatbreads, and top each with around 2 tbsps of tzatziki. Separate the onion pieces and tomatoes in equal amount and put them on the gyros.

*Nutritional values:*

Calories: 333 | Fat: 12.8 g | Sat. fat: 1.9 g | Mono fat: 4.8 g | Poly fat: 4.8 g | Protein: 22 g | Carbohydrate: 37 g | Fiber: 4 g | Cholesterol: 0.0 mg | Iron: 4 mg | Sodium: 722 mg | Calcium. 137 mg | Sugars: 3 g

## Dinner: slow cooker creamy lentil soup

Lentils are a plant-based cook's secret tool. Allow the carrot, lentil, and the onion mix to cook all day, after that throw in the chickpeas and kale in the last 30 mins before serving.

*Active ingredients:*

- Food preparation spray.
- 4 cups of reduced-sodium veggie brew.
- 1 cup of raw green lentils.
- 1 cup of sliced yellow onion.
- 3/4 cup of sliced carrots.
- 2 tsp of ground cumin.
- 1 tsp of kosher salt.
- 1/2 tsp of fresh ground black pepper.
- 5 thyme sprigs.
- 4 garlic cloves, diced.
- 1 (15-oz.) can of saltless chickpeas, rinsed and drained.
- 3/4 cup of water.
- 2 tbsp of olive oil.
- 1 tbsp of fresh lemon juice.
- 2 cups of very finely cut lacinato kale.
- 1/2 tsp of sherry or merlot vinegar.

*Exactly how to Make It:*

*Part 1*

Cover a 5- to 6-quart slow-moving cooker with oil spray. Place the brew in it and add all the 8 active ingredients (with garlic) in the slow-moving cooker; mix well. Cook with a lid on over low heat for about 7 hrs.

*Part 2*

Refine the chickpeas, 3/4 cup water, oil, and lemon juice in a mixer till smooth. Add the chickpea mix and kale to the rest of the ingredients already cooking and mix well.

*Nutritional values:*

Calories: 312 | Fat: 7 g | Sat. fat: 1 g | Unsat. fat: 5 g | Protein: 15 g | Carbohydrates: 47 g | Fiber: 12 g | Sugars: 5 g | Added sugars: 0 g | Sodium: 547 mg | Calcium: 12% DV | Potassium: 16% DV

## More plant-based recipes

## Wintertime greens salad with pomegranate & kumquats

*Ingredients:*

- 6 tbsp of pomegranate juice.
- 1/2 tsp of orange zest.
- 1 1/2 tbsp of orange juice.
- 1 1/2 tsp of corn starch.
- 1 1/2 tsp of sugar.
- ⅛ tsp of garlic salt.
- 1/4 cup of extra-virgin olive oil.
- 2 heads Belgian endive, cut, with leaves divided.
- 1 tiny head of radicchio, torn into tiny pieces.
- 5 cups of baby bitter greens, such as frisée, kale and/or arugula.
- 1 cup of pomegranate arils or raspberries.
- 1/2 cup of kumquats, very finely cut, or orange sectors.
- 1/4 cup of toasted walnuts.

- 1/4 cup of toasted pepitas or pistachio.

*Exactly how to make it:*

Incorporate the pomegranate juice, orange zest, orange juice, garlic, corn starch, sugar and salt in a tiny pan and blend well. Warm up over medium-high heat, mixing regularly, up until the blend starts to steam, reduces and becomes a lot clearer, it should take about 5 mins. Remove from the stove and allow it to cool at room temperature, for about 20 mins.

*Nutritional values:*

Per offering - Calories: 337 | Fat: 13 g (2 g rested) | Fiber: 6 g | Carbs: 28 | Healthy protein: 30 g | Folate: 91 mcg | Cholesterol: 62mg | Sugars: 16 g | Sugarcoated: 1 g | Vitamin A: 5,958 IU | Vitamin C: 80 mg | Calcium: 194 mg | Iron: 2 mg | Salt: 644 mg | Potassium: 860 mg

## Thai-style chopped salad with sriracha tofu

*Ingredients:*

- 1 (10 ounces) of salad mix.
- 1 (12 ounces) of edamame.
- 2 (7 ounces) of Flavored Baked Tofu, cubed.
- 1/2 cup of Spicy Peanut Vinaigrette.

*Exactly how to make it:*

Top each salad bowl with 1/2 cup edamame and a quarter of the tofu. Dress with vinaigrette up to 1 day before serving.

*Nutritional values:*

Per offering - Calories: 332 | Fat: 1 g (2 g rested) | Fiber: 8 g | Carbs: 26 g | Healthy protein: 27 g | Folate: 258 mcg | Sugars: 13 g | Sugarcoated: 4 g | Vitamin A: 2,085 IU | Vitamin C: 68 mg | Calcium: 0 mg | Iron: 4 mg | Salt: 236 mg | Potassium: 41 mg

## Vegan kale caesar salad with tofu croutons

*Ingredients for tofu croutons:*

- 1 (14 to 16 ounce) of extra-firm tofu, drained and cut into 3/4- inch dices.
- 1/4 cup of lemon juice.
- 1/4 cup of vegan Worcestershire sauce.
- 1 tsp of garlic powder.
- 1 tsp of onion powder.
- 3 tsp of olive oil.

*Salad:*

- 8 cups of cut Lacinato kale.
- 1/4 cup of dietary yeast.
- 1/4 cup of toasted pumpkin seeds.
- 1/2 cup of bottled vegan Caesar dressing.
- 1 avocado.

*Exactly how to make it:*

To prepare tofu croutons: Arrange the tofu on a baking sheet in between layers of paper towels. Allow it to stand for 15 mins or cool for up to 2 hrs. Put in each 1/2 cup of the croutons and 1 tbsp of pumpkin seeds.

For the salad: mix all the ingredients.

Serve the salad with the homemade croutons.

*Nutritional values:*

Per offering - Calories: 400 | Fat: 28 g ( 4 g rested) | Fiber: 9 g | Carbs: 19 g | Healthy protein: 20 g | Folate: 90 mcg | Cholesterol: 6 mg | Sugars: 2 g | Sugarcoated: 0 g | Vitamin A: 3,340 IU | Vitamin C: 51 mg | Calcium: 137 mg | Iron: 4 mg | Salt: 423 mg | Potassium: 670 mg

## Strawberry spinach salad with avocado & walnuts

*Ingredients:*

- 3 cups of baby spinach.
- 1 tbsp of carefully cut red onion.
- 1/2 cup of cut strawberries.
- 2 tbsp of vinaigrette.
- 1/4 medium avocado, diced.
- 2 tbsp of toasted walnut items.

*How to make it:*

Incorporate the spinach, the onion, and strawberries in a medium dish. Drizzle with the vinaigrette. Top with avocado and walnuts.

*Nutritional values:*

Per offering - Calories: 296 | Fat: 18 g ( 2 g rested) | Fiber: 10 g | Carbs. 27 g | Healthy protein: 8 g | Folate: 63 mcg | Cholesterol: 0 mg | Sugars: 11 g | Sugarcoated: 0 g | Vitamin A: 11,084 IU | Vitamin C:

103 mg | Calcium: 192 mg | Iron: 7 mg | Salt: 195 mg | Potassium: 385 mg

## Beefless vegan tacos

*Active ingredients:*

- 1 (16 ounces) bundle of extra-firm tofu, drained, crumbled and patted completely dry.
- 2 tbsp of reduced-sodium tamari or soy sauce.
- 1 tsp of chili powder.
- 1/2 tsp of garlic powder.
- 1/2 tsp of onion powder.
- 1 tbsp of extra-virgin olive oil.
- 1 ripe avocado.
- 1 tbsp of vegan mayo.
- 1 tsp of lime juice.
- Pinch of salt.
- 1/2 cup of fresh salsa or pico de gallo.
- 2 cups of shredded iceberg lettuce.
- 8 corn or flour tortillas, heated.
- Pickled radishes for garnish.

*How to make it:*

Mix the tofu, the tamari sauce (or soy sauce), chili powder, garlic powder and onion powder in a medium dish. Warm up the oil in a big nonstick frying pan over medium-high heat. Add the tofu mixture and cook it, stirring it sometimes, till it is perfectly browned. It should take between 8 to 10 mins.

*Nutritional values:*

Per offering - Calories: 360 | Fat: 21 g ( 3 g rested) Fiber: 8 g | Carbs: 33 g | Healthy protein: 17 g | Folate: 64 mcg | Cholesterol: 0 g | Sugars: 4 g | Sugarcoated: 0 g | Vitamin A: 556 IU | Vitamin C: 8 mg | Calcium: 375 mg | Iron: 4 mg | Salt: 610 mg | Potassium: 553 mg

## Curried sweet potato & peanut soup

*Ingredients:*

- 2 tbsp of canola oil.
- 1 1/2 cups of diced yellow onion.
- 1 tbsp of diced garlic.
- 1 tbsp of diced fresh ginger.
- 4 tsp of red curry paste.
- 1 serrano chili, seeds and ribs eliminated, diced.
- 1 extra pound of sweet potatoes, peeled off and diced (1/2- inch items).
- 3 cups of water.
- 1 cup of "lite" coconut milk.
- 3/4 cup of saltless dry-roasted peanuts.
- 1 (15 ounces) can white beans, washed.
- 3/4 tsp of salt.
- 1/4 tsp of ground pepper.
- 1/4 cup cut of fresh cilantro.
- 2 tbsp of lime juice.
- 1/4 cup of saltless baked pumpkin seeds.
- Lime wedges.

*How to make it:*

Add onion to a frying pan and cook them, mixing it a few times, up until they are softened and clear-looking, for about 4 mins. Mix in the garlic, ginger, curry paste, and serrano; cook, mixing occasionally, for 1 min. Decrease the heat to medium-low and simmer, partly covered, up until the sweet potatoes are soft. Cook for about 10 to 12 mins.

*Nutritional values:*

Per offering - Calories: 345 | Fat: 19 g ( 4 g rested) Fiber: 8 g | Carbs: 37 g | Healthy protein: 13 g | Folate: 95 mcg | Cholesterol: 0 g | Sugars: 7 g | Sugarcoated: 0 g | Vitamin A: 10,785 IU | Vitamin C: 8 mg | Calcium: 88 mg | Iron: 2 mg | Salt: 594 mg | Potassium: 699 mg

## Vegan superfood buddha bowls

*Ingredients:*

- 1 (8 ounces) bag microwavable quinoa.
- 1/2 cup of hummus.
- 2 tbsp of lemon juice.
- 1 (5 ounces) bundle baby kale leaves.
- 1 (8 ounces) of plain cooled prepared whole baby beetroots, cut (or 2 cups from a buffet).
- 1 cup of icy shelled edamame, defrosted.
- 1 medium avocado, cut.
- 1/4 cup saltless toasted sunflower seeds.

*How to make it:*

Slim the dressing down with water to the wanted consistency. Put in each bowl 1/2 cup of the quinoa, 1/2 cup beetroots, 1/4 cup edamame and 1 tbsp sunflower seeds. When it is all set to consume, add the 1/4 avocado and the hummus dressing.

*Nutritional values:*

Per offering - Calories: 381 | Fat: 19 g ( 2 g rested) Fiber: 13 g | Carbs: 43 g | Healthy protein: 16 g | Folate: 342 mcg | Cholesterol: 0 g | Sugars: 8 g | Sugarcoated: 0 g | Vitamin A: 3,764 IU | Vitamin C: 55 mg | Calcium: 126 mg | Iron: 5 mg | Salt: 188 mg | Potassium: 1,066 mg

## Apricot-spinach salad

*Active ingredients:*

- 1 (15 ounces) can of black beans, rinsed and drained.
- 1/2 cup cut of dried out apricots.
- 1 medium yellow or red bell pepper, cut into strips.
- 1 scallion, very finely cut.
- 1 tbsp of sliced fresh cilantro.
- 1 garlic clove, diced.
- 1/4 cup of apricot nectar.
- 2 tbsp of salad oil.
- 2 tbsp of rice vinegar.
- 1 tsp of reduced-sodium soy sauce.
- 1 tsp of grated fresh ginger.
- 4 cups of shredded fresh spinach.

*Exactly how to make it:*

Put in a dish the ingredients delicately to form layers. Cover with some aluminum foil and cool for 2 to 24 hrs. Top with a black bean mix.

*Nutritional values:*

Per offering - Calories: 211 | Fat: 7 g ( 1 g rested) Fiber: 8 g | Carbs: 33 g | Healthy protein: 9 g | Folate: 80 mcg | Cholesterol: 0 g |

Sugars: 10 g | Sugarcoated: 0 g | Vitamin A: 6,204 IU | Vitamin C: 60 mg | Calcium: 84 mg | Iron: 3 mg | Salt: 336 mg | Potassium: 780 mg

## Fundamental black beans

*Ingredients:*

- 1 extra pound of dried out black beans.
- 1 onion, quartered.
- 1 head of garlic, leading 3rd cut to subject cloves.
- 2 dried out bay fallen leaves.
- 1 tsp of kosher salt.

*Exactly how to make it:*

Choose any kind of beans you like, after that wash them under cold water and transfer to a big dish. Drain and rinse the beans again and after that transfer them to a big pot or Dutch stove and cover with at least 2 inches of water. Cook until they are soft. Using a slotted spoon, move the beans to an offering bowl or container to store the beans in the fridge.

*Nutritional values:*

Per offering - Calories: 155 | Fat: 1 g ( 0 g rested) Fiber: 7 g | Carbs: 28 g | Healthy protein: 10 g | Folate: 201 mcg | Cholesterol: 0 g | Sugars: 1 g | Sugarcoated: 0 g | Vitamin A: 8 IU | Vitamin C: 0 mg | Calcium: 56 mg | Iron: 2 mg | Salt: 114 mg | Potassium: 673 mg

## Vegan chicken nuggets

*Ingredients:*

- 16 ounces of seitan.
- 1/4 cup of vegan mayo.
- 6 tsp of water.
- 1/2 tsp of fowl flavoring.
- 3/4 cup of whole-wheat breadcrumbs.

*How to make it:*

Cut the seitan into 16 (1/2 inch) nuggets. Blend the fowl seasoning, the mayo and water in a pie plate. Coat the seitan and bake it, removing it from the oven as soon as it gets gently browned on both sides, it should take about 18 to 20 mins.

To make in advance: Freeze prepared nuggets in a closed container for approximately 1 month. To offer, reheat the seitan in the microwave or on the stove.

*Nutritional values:*

Per offering - Calories: 306 | Fat: 12 g ( 2 g rested) Fiber: 5 g | Carbs: 19 g | Healthy protein: 29 g | Folate: 129 mcg | Cholesterol: 0 g | Sugars: 2 g | Sugarcoated: 0 g | Vitamin A: 6 IU | Vitamin C: 0 mg | Calcium: 61 mg | Iron: 3 mg | Salt: 388 mg | Potassium: 247 mg

## Sopa tarasca

*Components:*

- 1 extra pound of dried out pinto beans, soaked overnight.
- 2 tbsp of canola oil.
- 1 1/2 cups of diced onions.
- 4 garlic cloves, diced.
- 2 tsp of ground cumin.
- 1 tsp of chili powder.

- 6 cups of water.
- 3 dried out ancho chiles, seeded and stemmed.
- 1 (28 ounces) can of whole tomatoes.
- 1 tsp of salt.
- 1/4 tsp of ground pepper.
- 1 ripe avocado, cut.
- Crumbled queso fresco, lime wedges & tortilla chips for garnish.

*Exactly how to make it:*

Drain the cans of beans and wash them. Add the drained beans and water in a pan. Add the chilis, the tomatoes and salt, pepper and juice to the beans.

*Nutritional values:*

Per offering - Calories: 339 | Fat: 9 g ( 1 g rested) Fiber: 14 g | Carbs: 48 g | Healthy protein: 15 g | Folate: 336 mcg | Cholesterol: 0 g | Sugars: 5 g | Sugarcoated: 0 g | Vitamin A: 1,847 IU | Vitamin C: 21 mg | Calcium: 124 mg | Iron: 5 mg | Salt: 433 mg | Potassium: 1,314 mg

## Homemade seitan

*Active ingredients:*

- 2 cups of wheat gluten.
- 1/2 cup of dietary yeast.
- 2 tsp of dried out minced garlic.
- 2 tsp of dried out minced onion.
- 4 cups of low-sodium veggie brew, split.
- 2 tbsp of white miso .

- 4 pieces of ginger.

*Exactly how to make it:*

Blend 1 cup of brew and miso in a medium dish (or a big bowl); add the completely dry ingredients blended together. Mix on a medium-low heat up it becomes elastic, for about 3 mins (or mix it by hand in the dish up until it is flexible, for 3 to 5 mins), adding even more brew if the dough is too dry. Reduce heat to medium-low, cover with a lid and cook up until it becomes firm, for about 30 mins.

*Nutritional values:*

Per offering - Calories: 162 | Fat: 1 g ( 0 g rested) Fiber: 3 g | Carbs: 10 g | Healthy protein: 27 g | Folate: 120 mcg | Cholesterol: 0 g | Sugars: 1 g | Sugarcoated: 0 g | Vitamin A: 0 IU | Vitamin C: 0 mg | Calcium: 25 mg | Iron: 2 mg | Salt: 211 mg | Potassium: 192 mg

## Thai spaghetti squash with peanut sauce

*Components:*

- 1 2 1/2- to 3-pound of pasta squash, halved lengthwise and seeded.
- 1/2 cup of smooth all-natural peanut butter.
- 1/4 cup of reduced-sodium tamari or soy sauce.
- 1/4 cup of water.
- 1 tbsp of rice vinegar.
- 1 tbsp of syrup.
- 1 tsp of diced garlic.
- 1/4- 1/2 tsp of smashed red pepper.
- 1 cup of icy shelled edamame, defrosted.

- 1/2 cup of very finely cut red bell pepper, halved crosswise.
- 1 medium carrot, shredded.
- 1/4 cup of cut scallions.
- 1/4 cup of cut saltless baked peanuts.
- 1/4 cup of sliced fresh cilantro.
- Lime wedges for offering.

*Exactly how to make it:*

Place fifty percent of the squash, cut-side down, in a microwave-safe dish; add 2 tbsps of water. Microwave without anything covering it on High up until the flesh is tender, for about 10 to 15 mins. When the squash has cooled down, add the edamame, the bell pepper, the carrot and the scallions to the dish.

*Nutritional values:*

Per offering - Calories: 419 | Fat: 24 g ( 4 g rested) Fiber: 9 g | Carbs: 33 g | Healthy protein: 18 g | Folate: 170 mcg | Cholesterol: 0 g | Sugars: 13 g | Sugarcoated: 3 g | Vitamin A: 3,664 IU | Vitamin C: 33 mg | Calcium: 93 mg | Iron: 3 mg | Salt: 856 mg | Potassium: 568 mg

## Vegan burrito bowls with cauliflower rice

*Ingredients:*

- 1 (12 ounces) plain icy riced cauliflower.
- 4 tsp of olive oil.
- 1 tsp of no-salt-added taco spices.
- 1 cup of very finely cut red cabbage.
- 1 cup of diced avocado.

- 1/2 cup of pico de gallo or salsa.
- 1/4 cup of sliced fresh cilantro.

*Beefless ground beef:*

- 1 (16 ounces) of plain extra-firm tofu, drained, crumbled and patted completely dry.
- 2 tbsp of tamari.
- 1/2 tsp of garlic powder.
- 1/2 tsp of paprika.
- 1 tbsp of extra-virgin olive oil.

*How to make it:*

While the Beefless Ground Beef cooks, prepare riced cauliflower according to the package instructions. Separate the cauliflower amongst 4 single-serving containers with covers. Cover each with 1/2 cup of Beefless Ground Beef, 1/4 cup each of cabbage and some avocado, 2 tbsps of pico de gallo (or salsa) and 1 tbsp of cilantro.

*Beefless hamburger:*

Incorporate the tofu, the tamari, garlic powder and paprika in a tool dish. Warm up the oil in a huge nonstick frying pan over medium-high heat. Add the tofu combination and cook, mixing periodically, up until the tofu is perfectly browned, 8 to 10 mins.

*Nutritional values:*

Per offering - Calories: 152 | Fat: 9 g ( 1 g rested) Fiber: 2 g | Carbs: 4 g | Healthy protein: 13 g | Folate: 0 mcg | Cholesterol: 0 g | Sugars: 0 g | Sugarcoated: 3 g | Vitamin A: 184 IU | Vitamin C: 0 mg | Calcium: 98 mg | Iron: 2 mg | Salt: 500 mg | Potassium: 11 mg

. . .

## Vegan freezer breakfast burritos

*Components:*

- 2 tbsp of avocado oil.
- 1 (14 ounces) plain extra-firm water-packed tofu, drained and crumbled.
- 2 tsp of chili powder.
- 1 tsp of ground cumin.
- 1/4 tsp of salt.
- 1 (15 ounces) can reduced-sodium black beans, washed.
- 1 cup of icy corn, defrosted.
- 4 scallions, cut.
- 1/2 cup of ready fresh salsa.
- 1/4 cup of cut fresh cilantro.
- 6 (8 inches) whole-wheat tortillas or covers.

*How to make it:*

Warm up 1 tbsp of oil in a huge nonstick frying pan over medium heat. Include another 1 tbsp oil to the frying pan. Add the salsa and the cilantro; cook, mixing sometimes, till it is all heated up, for about 2 mins. Add the tofu and the spices to a frying pan and cook till it's golden in color. Assemble your burrito!

*Nutritional values:*

Per offering - Calories: 329 | Fat: 10 g ( 2 g rested) Fiber: 8 g | Carbs: 45 g | Healthy protein: 15 g | Folate: 48 mcg | Cholesterol: 0 g | Sugars: 5 g | Sugarcoated: 0 g | Vitamin A: 565 IU | Vitamin C: 4 mg | Calcium: 286 mg | Iron: 4 mg | Salt: 665 mg | Potassium: 423 mg

## Tofu & snow pea stir-fry with peanut sauce

*Ingredients:*

- 1/3 cup of saltless all-natural peanut butter.
- 3 tbsp of rice vinegar.
- 2 tbsp of low-sodium soy sauce.
- 2 tips of brow sugar.
- 2 tsp of warm sauce, such as Sriracha.
- 1 (14 ounces) bundle extra-firm or company tofu.
- 4 tsp of canola oil.
- 1 (14 ounces) bundle icy (not defrosted) pepper stir-fry veggies.
- 2 tbsp of carefully sliced or grated fresh ginger.
- 3 garlic cloves, diced.
- 2 cups of fresh snow peas, cut.
- 2 tbsp of water, plus more if required.
- 4 tbsp of saltless baked peanuts.
- 2 cups of prepared wild rice.

*How to make it:*

In a bowl combine the peanut butter, vinegar, soy sauce, sugar, and hot sauce in a medium bowl and mix until everything is smooth. Set aside for later.

In a nonstick frying pan over medium heat add the tofu and let it cook for two minutes. Then stir and let it cook until it has browned. Transfer to a plate and set aside for later

Add more oil to the pan and mix in the vegetables plus the spices and cook until everything is soft. Add the peanut butter and stir for 30 seconds. Lastly, add the tofu.

Serve with the rice.

*Nutritional values:*

Per offering - Calories: 514 | Fat: 27 g ( 4 g rested) Fiber: 7 g |

Carbs: 49 g | Healthy protein: 22 g | Folate: 40 mcg | Cholesterol: 0 g | Sugars: 12 g | Sugarcoated: 3 g | Vitamin A: 1,331 IU | Vitamin C: 13 mg | Calcium: 136 mg | Iron: 4 mg | Salt: 376 mg | Potassium: 319 mg

## Vegan meatballs

For these healthy and balanced, plant-based vegan meatballs, we've switched out the typical hamburger and pork for protein-packed chickpeas and quinoa - without sparing any one of those Italian tastes that you try to find in a traditional meatball. Mushrooms up the umami aspect and a basic tomato sauce finishes the picture. Offer over your preferred pasta.

*Active ingredients:*

- 2 1/2 cups of tiny cauliflower florets.
- 8 ounces of white mushrooms, cut in half.
- 1/2 little onion, coarsely sliced.
- 2 huge garlic cloves, diced.
- 4 tbsp of extra-virgin olive oil.
- 1 1/2 tsp of Italian spices,.
- 1/2 tsp of salt.
- 1/4 tsp of ground pepper.
- 1 tbsp of tomato paste.
- 1 cup of tinned chickpeas.
- 2 cups of prepared quinoa.
- 1 tbsp of reduced-sodium tamari or soy sauce.
- 1 (28 ounces) can of no-salt-added smashed tomatoes.
- 1/2 tsp of smashed red pepper.
- 2 tbsp of cut fresh basil.

*How to make it:*

Clean the cauliflower, mushrooms, onion and 1 garlic clove carefully sliced in a food cup, for about 15 minutes. Include the tomato and prepare and paste, mixing, for 1 min. Include the chickpea combination to the dish along with the quinoa and the tamari (or soy sauce); mix to integrate.

To make in advance: The sauce can be made up to 3 days in advance, and the meatballs can be made 1 day in advance. Cool individually.

*Nutritional values:*

Per offering - Calories: 394 | Fat: 17 g ( 2 g rested) Fiber: 10 g | Carbs: 46 g | Healthy protein: 13 g | Folate: 102 mcg | Cholesterol: 0 g | Sugars: 12 g | Sugarcoated: 0 g | Vitamin A: 1,865 IU | Vitamin C: 47 mg | Calcium: 59 mg | Iron: 6 mg | Salt: 434 mg | Potassium: 1,272 mg

## Thai tofu & vegetable curry with zucchini noodles

For this fast Thai curry dish, we've integrated tofu and lots of veggies with a tasty sauce made with red curry paste, lime juice and coconut milk. Offer the curry over gently heated zucchini noodles. Perks: Everything is prepared in one frying pan, so there's just one frying pan to clean after supper.

*Active ingredients:*

- 2 tbsp of toasted sesame oil.
- 1 (14 ounces) plain extra-firm tofu, cut into pieces of 1/2-inch-thickness.
- 1 (14 ounces) can of coconut milk.
- 2 tbsp of red curry paste.
- 1 tbsp of lime juice.

- 2 medium garlic clove, grated.
- 1/2 tsp of salt.
- 1 tbsp of avocado oil.
- 1 (8 ounces) bundle of cut mushrooms.
- 1 lot of scallions, cut into 1-inch pieces.
- 6 cups of cut kale.
- 2 (10 ounce) bundles of zucchini noodles.

*How to make it:*

Rub the tofu completely dry and put it in a frying pan. Add kale, the sauce mix and the tofu and cook. After the kale has shriveled, the sauce has thickened, and the tofu is heated up (it will take about 2 mins) add the zucchini noodles. Cook, gently mixing, for about one minute.

*Nutritional values:*

Per offering - Calories: 428 | Fat: 37 g ( 21 g rested) Fiber: 5 g | Carbs: 17 g | Healthy protein: 16 g | Folate: 125 mcg | Cholesterol: 0 g | Sugars: 7 g | Sugarcoated: 0 g | Vitamin A: 2,907 IU | Vitamin C: 62 mg | Calcium: 297 mg | Iron: 6 mg | Salt: 518 mg | Potassium: 1,106 mg

## Green lentil curry masabacha

*Active ingredients:*

- 3 tbsp of extra-virgin olive oil 1 tiny onion, carefully diced.
- 1 1/2 tsp of diced garlic.
- 2/3 cup of green lentils, washed.
- 2/3 cup of red lentils, washed.

- 2 cups of low-sodium no-chicken or poultry brew.
- 1-2 cups of water.
- 1 1/2 tsp of curry powder.
- 1 medium carrot, coarsely grated.
- 1/4 tsp of kosher salt.
- 1/4 tsp of ground pepper.
- 1 cup of very finely cut arugula.
- 2 tbsp of carefully sliced red onion.
- 1 jalapeño pepper, cut.

*Tahini Sauce:*

- 2/3 cup of tahini.
- 1 1/2 tsp of diced garlic.
- 1/2 cup of ice water.
- 1/4 cup of lemon juice.
- 1/4 tsp of kosher salt.

*How to make it:*

Put garlic in a frying pan with a bit of oil for 1 min and let it golden. Add the red and green lentils, brew, 1 cup water and add curry powder. Then add all the tahini sauce ingredients to a mixer and refine till the tahini is smooth. Transfer the tahini to the frying pan and let it cook until the sauce is heated up and light, for about 1 min.

*Nutritional values:*

Per offering - Calories: 402 | Fat: 19 g ( 3 g rested) Fiber: 8 g | Carbs: 44 g | Healthy protein: 17 g | Folate: 95 mcg | Cholesterol: 0 g | Sugars: 4 g | Sugarcoated: 0 g | Vitamin A: 2,735 IU | Vitamin C: 17 mg | Calcium: 82 mg | Iron: 5 mg | Salt: 414 mg | Potassium: 427 mg

. . .

### High-protein plant-based meals recipes

## Apple pie smoothie

*Components for 4 portions:*

- 4 Apples.
- 17 oz of coconut yogurt.
- 4 cups of almond milk.
- 4 tbsp of chia seeds.
- 2.1 oz of rolled oats.
- 1 tsp of ground cinnamon.
- 4 scoops of vanilla, vegan healthy protein powder.
- 1 tsp of ground nutmeg.
- If your healthy protein powder is fairly sweetened you will not require this, 1 tsp stevia (optional).

*How to make it:*

Separate the completely dry active ingredients right into bags or containers for easy early morning access. Freeze your apples so no piece gets bad before you can eat them!

When it is morning time, take as many apple pieces as you want and put them into a blender or food processor with the almond milk, coconut yogurt and the prepped container of completely dry components.

Mix up until it is smooth and then you just need to enjoy it!

*Nutritional values:*

Calories: 485 | Protein: 36g | Fat: 14 g | Carbs: 54 g | Sodium: 593 mg | Fiber: 12 g | Sugar: 19 g

. . .

# Spicy peanut butter tempeh & rice

*Active ingredients for 4 portions:*

*Cornerstone:*

- 22 oz of Tempeh, cut into 1-inch dices.
- 6.5 oz of wild rice, raw.
- Coconut oil spray.

*Sauce:*

- 4 tbsp of peanut butter.
- 4 tbsp of soy sauce (reduced salt).
- 4 tsp of coconut sugar.
- 2 tbsp of red chili sauce.
- 2 tsp of rice vinegar.
- 2 tbsp of ginger (fresh or paste).
- 3 cloves of garlic (or garlic paste).
- 6 tbsp of water.

*Cabbage:*

- 5 oz of purple cabbage, shaved/finely cut.
- 1 Lime, juice just.
- 2 tsp of agave/apple bee-free honey.
- 3 tsp of sesame oil.

*Garnish:*

- Green onion, cut.

*How to make it:*

Mix every one of the ingredients for the spicy peanut sauce with each other.

Cut the tempeh into 1-inch (2.5 centimeters) dices.

Add the sauce to the tempeh, mix and marinade, putting it in the refrigerator to let it rest for 2-3 hrs after having covered it with tinfoil or, preferably, overnight. In this way, the tempeh will be able to absorb all the flavors of the sauce.

Preheat the stove to 375 ° F/190 ° C cook the rice based on the package guidelines.

Put the tempeh on a nonstick flat pan, spray with some coconut oil, cook on the stove for 25-30 mins. Conserve any kind remanence of the sauce for the last touches to the dish.

Mix every ingredient with the cabbage in a dish and put it aside for a while to allow it to get well seasoned.

Offer it up: add to a dish or a container the tempeh, the rice and the cabbage. Drizzle on top the rest of the marinade sauce. Garnish with sliced green onion.

*Nutritional values:*

Calories: 608 | Protein: 43 g | Fat: 24 g | Carbs: 56 g | Sodium: 860 mg | Fiber: 5 g | Sugar: 12 g

**Eco-friendly protein snack pot**

*Components for 4 portions:*

- 8 oz of edamame beans, iced up.
- 8 oz of peas, iced up.
- 4 tbsp of sesame seeds.
- 4 tbsp of soy sauce (with reduced salt).
- Chili sauce/Sriracha as favored, to taste.
- Cilantro, optional.

*How to make it:*

Put some icy peas and edamame in a microwave-safe dish. Include a sprinkle of water and let them defrost in the microwave for around 30 secs or until they are no longer frozen.

In a little pot or container, place the seeds together with the beans and peas.

Mix with soy chili, sauce and cilantro prior to consuming. Dig in!

*Nutritional values:*

Calories: 177 | Protein: 11 g | Fat: 8 g | Carbs: 16 g | Sodium: 994 mg | Fiber: 7 g | Sugar: 7 g

## Italian veggie "meatballs" & spaghetti

*Components for 4 portions:*

*Veggie-meatballs:*

- 13 oz of kidney beans, drained and washed.
- 12 oz of vegetable ground.
- 3 tbsp of whole wheat breadcrumbs.
- 3 tbsp of grated flaxseed.
- 6 tbsp of water.

*Flavoring:*

- 1.5 tbsp of Italian spices.
- 1 tbsp of garlic powder.
- 3 tbsp of fresh parsley, sliced.

*Various other components:*

- 16 oz marinara.
- 7 oz whole wheat spaghetti.
- Olive oil spray.

*How to prepare it:*

Preheat the oven at 400° F/ 200° C mix the flaxseed and water with each other in a little dish.

Place the beans in a food mill and mix it until it becomes smooth.

Mix all the active meatball ingredients in a dish and then add all the flax seeds and the beans. Include the flavorings. Form your meatballs.

Put the meatballs in the refrigerator or freezer, cool for at least 20 minutes, and afterward put them the stove. This will help them tighten up and prevent them from falling apart while you are eating them.

Spray a cooking sheet with olive oil, include the balls to the tray. Spray with olive oil and then place it on the stove for 20 mins.

Prepare your pasta as per package directions in a pot of steaming salty water. As soon as it is prepared, drain the pasta.

In a different frying pan, warm up the marinara sauce and include the meatballs as quickly as they are ready.

Serve the pasta with the juicy vegetable meatballs on the top.

*Nutritional values:*

Calories: 498 | Protein: 36 g | Fat: 12 g | Carbs: 61 g | Sodium: 464 mg | Fiber: 16 g | Sugar: 7 g

## Vegan fry-up

*Active ingredients:*

*For the hash browns:*

- 1 huge potato, unpeeled.
- 1 1/2 tbsp of peanut butter.

*For the mushrooms and tomatoes:*

- 14 cherry tomatoes
- Sunflower oil
- 2 tsp of syrup
- 1 tsp of soy sauce
- 1/4 tsp f smoked paprika
- 1 big Portobello mushroom, cut

*For the clambered tofu:*

- 349 g pack of silken tofu.
- 2 tbsp of dietary yeast.
- 1/2 tsp of turmeric extract.
- 1 garlic clove, squashed.

*To offer:*

- 4 vegan sausages (we utilized Dee's leek & onion).
- 1 x 200g can of baked beans.

*How to make it:*

Prepare the potato by putting it whole in a huge saucepan full of water and boil it for 10 minutes; after that drain the pot and let the boiled potato cool down. Smash the potato and mix it well with the peanut butter.

Warmth stove to 200C/180C. Place the cherry tomatoes onto a cooking tray, drizzle with 2 tsp of sunflower oil, mix and cook for 30 minutes or till the skins have blistered and have begun to char. Prepare the sausages and beans by adhering to the directions on the pack, so they're prepared to offer at the same time as the tofu.

Blend the maple syrup, soy sauce and 1/4 tsp of smoked paprika with each other in a big dish, include the sliced-up mushrooms. Leave to rest while you put 2 tsp of sunflower oil into a nonstick frying pan and bring it up to medium-high heat.

Place 1 tablespoon oil into the frying pan and add the potato mixture - you should get about 4 layers - fry for 3-4 minutes each side and after that drain the of excessive oil with kitchen paper.

Put the tofu into the frying pan and spray over the heat and sprinkle a pinch of salt and pepper. If the frying pan looks a little too dry add little a bit of oil. Fry for 3 to 4 minutes or till the tofu is well cooked, well covered in the spices and warm.

Separate the food in between 2 plates and offer with a warm cup of tea with soy milk, if used.

*Nutritional values:*

Calories: 644 | Fat: 26 g | Fills: 4 g | Carbohydrates: 56 g | Sugars: 19 g | Fiber: 11g | Healthy protein: 41 g | Salt: 3.11 g

## Seitan

*Active ingredients:*

- 250 g firm tofu.
- 150 ml unsweetened soy milk.
- 2 tsp of miso paste.
- 2 tsp of marmite.
- 1 tsp of onion powder.
- 2 tsp of garlic powder.
- 160 g of wheat gluten.

- 40 g of pea healthy protein or vegan healthy protein powder.
- 1 1/2 liters of veggie broth.

*How to make it:*

Put the tofu, soy milk, miso, Marmite, onion powder, garlic powder, 1 tsp salt and 1/2 tsp white pepper in a food mill and blend till smooth.

After this put into a dish, the wheat gluten and healthy pea protein or healthy protein powder. As soon as the ingredients of the dough have combined with each other, knead it, tearing and extending it for 10-15 minutes.

Put the veggie broth into a frying pan. Simmer it for 20 minutes, covered with a lid, after that let it cool down. When you are ready to serve the seitan in a dish, rub it completely dry with a cooking paper towel and after that cut smaller sized pieces.

*Nutritional values:*

Calories: 173 | Calories from Fat: 12 | Fat: 1.3 g | Saturated Fat: 0.1 g | Sodium: 562 mg | Potassium: 127 mg | Carbohydrates: 15.2 g | Fiber 2.2 g | Sugar: 1.7 g | Protein: 25.9 g

## Seitan & black bean stir-fry

*Active ingredients:*

For the sauce:

- 400 g can of black beans, drained and washed.
- 75 g of dark brown soft sugar.
- 3 garlic cloves.

- 2 tbsp of soy sauce.
- 1 tsp of Chinese five-spice powder.
- 2 tbsp of rice vinegar.
- 1 tbsp of smooth peanut butter.
- 1 red chili carefully sliced.

For the stir-fry:

- 350 g of marinated seitan pieces (we made use of Biona).
- 1 tbsp of corn flour.
- 2-3 tbsp of oil.
- 1 red pepper, cut.
- 300 g of pak choi, cut.
- 2 springtime onions, cut.
- prepared rice noodles or rice, to offer.

*How to make it:*

Begin by preparing the sauce, pour half the beans into a dish of a food mill with the rest of the ingredients and add 50ml water. After that mix up until smooth. Pour into a pan and heat it delicately for about 5 minutes or till it has become shiny and has thickened.

Warm up your frying pan to a high temperature level, add a little oil, and after that, add the seitan - you could require to do this in sets. Stir-fry for around 5 minutes up until the seitan get gold brownish at the sides.

If the frying pan is completely dry at this phase, add 1 tbsp vegetable oil. Cook for 3-4 minutes, and after that return, the seitan to the frying pan, mix in the sauce and bring to a boil for 1 minute.

*Nutritional values:*

Calories: 326 | Fat: 8 g | Fills: 1 g | Carbohydrates: 37 g | Sugars: 23 g | Fiber: 7 g | Healthy protein: 22 g | Salt 3.08 g

. . .

## Curried tofu covers

*Components:*

- 1/2 red cabbage (regarding 500g), shredded.
- 4 loaded tablespoons of dairy-free yogurt (we utilized Alpro Level with Coconut).
- 3 tablespoons of mint sauce.
- 3 x 200 g packs of tofu, each cut into 15 dices.
- 2 tablespoons of tandoori curry paste.
- 2 tablespoons of oil.
- 2 onions, cut.
- 2 big garlic cloves, cut.
- 8 chapatis.
- 2 limes, cut into quarters.

*Exactly how to make it:*

Mix in the tofu with the tandoori paste and 1 tablespoon of the oil into a frying pan. Warm up the frying pan and cook the tofu, in sets, for a couple of minutes until each side is golden. Add the rest of the oil to the frying pan, mix in the onions and garlic, and cook for 8-10 minutes up until softened.

Warm up the chapatis adhering to the pack guidelines. Serve the chapatis in a bowl with the tofu and after that add some cabbage, with by the curried tofu and a squeeze of lime.

*Nutritional values:*

Calories: 128 | Calories from Fat: 45 | Fat: 5 g | Fills: 5 g | Saturated Fat: 1 g | Polyunsaturated Fat: 1 g | Sodium: 303 mg | Potassium: 53 mg | Carbohydrates: 15 g | Fiber: 4 g | Sugar: 9 g | Protein: 7 g

**Vegan covered dish**

*Active ingredients:*

- 1 tbsp of olive or rapeseed oil.
- 1 onion, carefully sliced.
- 3 garlic cloves, cut.
- 1 tsp of smoked paprika.
- 1/2 tsp of ground cumin.
- 1 tbsp of dried out thyme.
- 3 medium carrots, cut (about 200g).
- 2 medium celery sticks, carefully cut (about 120g).
- 1 red pepper, sliced.
- 1 yellow pepper, sliced.
- 2 x 400 g of canisters tomatoes or peeled off cherry tomatoes.
- 1 veggie stock dice mixed with 250ml of water (we made use of 1 Knorr veggie supply pot).
- 2 courgettes, cut heavily (regarding 300g).
- 2 sprigs of fresh thyme.
- 250 g of prepared lentils.

*How to make it:*

Warm up 1 tablespoon of olive or rapeseed oil in a big, heavy-based frying pan. Add 1 carefully cut onion and cook it for 5 - 10 minutes till it has softened.

Add 3 sliced up garlic cloves, 1 tsp of smoked paprika, 1/2 tsp of ground cumin, 1 tablespoon of dried out thyme, 3 chopped carrots, 2 carefully cut celery sticks, 1 cut red pepper and 1 sliced yellow pepper and cook for 5 mins.

Add 2 400g canisters of tomatoes, 250ml veggie broth (made with 1 stock), 2 roughly cut courgettes and 2 sprigs of fresh thyme and cook for 20 - 25 mins.

Secure the thyme sprigs. Mix in 250g of the prepared lentils and bring to a simmer. Offer with white basmati mash, quinoa or rice.

*Nutritional values.*

Calories: 216 | Fat: 5.1 g | Fills: 0.7 g | Carbohydrates: 31g | Sugars: 16.1 g | Fiber: 9.8 g | Healthy protein: 12.3 g | Salt: 1.6 g

## Sticky tofu with *noodles*

*Ingredients*:

- 1/2 huge cucumber.
- 100ml of rice red wine vinegar.
- 2 tbsp of gold wheel sugar.
- 100ml of oil.
- 200 g pack of firm tofu, cut into 3cm dices.
- 2 tbsp of syrup.
- 4 tbsp of white or brownish miso paste.
- 30 g of white sesame seeds.
- 250 g of dried out soba noodles.
- 2 spring onions, shredded, to offer.

*Exactly how to make it:*

Using a peeler, cut slim strings off the cucumber, leaving the seeds behind. Place the bows in a dish and put it aside for later. Delicately warm up the vinegar, sugar, 1/4 tsp of salt and 100ml of water in a pan over a small flame for 3-5 minutes up until the sugar lique-fies. After that pour in the cucumbers and put to marinade in the refrigerator while you prepare the tofu.

Add the tofu to a frying pan and fry for 7-10 minutes, increasing temperature midway, up until the tofu has gold brownish color on each side. Brush the fried tofu with the sticky honey sauce and put aside any leftover. Cover the tofu uniformly in the seeds, sprinkle a little bit of salt and then leave it in a warm location.

Return the frying pan to the stove, throw in the noodles with the rest of the oil, the sauce and 1 tablespoon of the cucumber marinade. Separate the noodles in between bowls and top them with the tofu, few strings of marinated cucumber and the spring onion.

*Nutritional values:*

Calories: 972 | Fat: 35 g | Fills: 2 g | Carbohydrates: 113 g | Sugars: 12g | Fiber: 6 g | Healthy protein: 50 g | Salt: 5.3 g

# CHAPTER 14: MYTHS ABOUT PROTEIN AND A PLANT-BASED DIET

Healthy protein has ended up being commonly acknowledged as a wonder macronutrient that is still being tested for obtaining its right dosage. Allow me to make some clarification on a few plant-based healthy proteins' most-common mistaken beliefs:

## Misconception # 1: The more protein, the better

Human beings do, without a doubt, call for healthy protein, as it is one of the 3 macronutrients, and we require to acquire it from our diet plan. When it comes to healthy protein, eating an unwanted amount of what we need might lead to illnesses.

The United States Department of Agriculture's Recommended Daily Allowance for healthy protein is 0.7 grams per kilo of body weight per day for individuals older than 19 years of age. Several individuals are taking in around 20 to 30 percent of their calories from healthy protein, which equates to 90 to 135 grams of healthy protein on a 1,800-calorie diet plan (regular women consumption) and 125 to 188 grams of healthy protein on a 2,500-calorie diet plan (regular male consumption). Much of this excess of healthy protein comes from animal resources, which might be specifically harmful.

## Misconception # 2: "Complete proteins" are hard to find

One vital factor this misconception lays on is the fact that since the amino acids - the structure blocks of healthy protein - are present in animal produces in a way that is much more similar to the way they are present in our body. When you eat any kind of healthy protein, it is broken down using food digestive enzymes into its different amino acid components and is merged in the blood for additional usage. When the body requires to have a healthy protein for an enzyme or to fix muscle mass cells, it accumulates the needed for amino acids and strings them back with each other in the series suitable for what it is presently producing.

Despite this, plant healthy protein is flawlessly packaged along with a wealth of phytonutrients, antioxidants, vitamins, minerals, and fiber - all important parts for ideal health and wellness and risk prevention. On the contrary, healthy animal protein is covered up with undesirable saturated fat and nutritional cholesterol.

## Misconception # 3: The more active you are, the more protein you need

All whole plant foods have at least a small quantity of protein, so if you take a sufficient amount and a selection of entire plant foods, your healthy protein demand will conveniently be satisfied. Professional athletes have boosted total calorie needs, so when they increase their consumption of whole plant foods, they immediately fulfill their better demand for all the macronutrients, consisting of healthy protein, carbs, and fats.

When it is about healthy protein, it is not concerning taking in as much as we can, it is instead about eating the correct amount. Whole plant foods, as given in nature, provide an excellent quantity of healthy protein essential for the development, the upkeep, and the work of metabolic procedures.

# CHAPTER 15: HOW I GET 80 GRAMS OF PROTEIN A DAY WITHOUT EATING MEAT (MY PERSONAL EXPERIENCE)

There are many viewpoints available concerning healthy protein - just how much you ought to be consuming and when you must be consuming it - and everybody (yes, I indicate every person) has a point of view concerning non-meat-eaters obtaining their healthy protein. Undoubtedly one of the most usual questions to a person claiming they do not consume meat is "Where/how do you obtain your healthy protein?"

I've invested the last 11 years of my life as a vegan - attempting every various level of plant-based diets, from vegan to ovo-vegetarian, to pescatarian. At each degree, I've needed to consider where I'm obtaining my healthy protein and although I like veggies, I cannot get the healthy protein quantities I require to recuperate from my exercises by consuming just vegetables (for the recommendation, 1 cup of vegetables typically has 2 to 5 grams of healthy protein). And while there are a lot of clashing healthy protein viewpoints available, my perspective is straightforward: if you have a healthy protein objective, you need to have a healthy and balanced alternative to aid you to reach your needs, no matter what that number is.

Today, I go for 60 to 80 grams of healthy protein a day. It might appear high, however, this number was established for me by a naturopathic physician, picked especially for my body and exercise program (which is very important since, according to Will Cole, D.C., the quantity of healthy protein a person needs to consume each day depends upon lots of aspects such as their body mass, weight, and active they are). Certainly, it is simpler to get 60 grams than 80, however, I change it as my body requires, primarily relying on just how starving I am, and the effort put in my workouts.

If you are looking to increase your healthy protein consumption or only looking for a plant-based healthy protein inspiration, below are some techniques that have used and helped me reach that number more easily (without, of course, consuming meat).

## 1. I constantly begin my day with a protein-filled dish

Up until I had a healthy protein objective, my breakfast was a rather low-protein dish for me. I used to consume oatmeal with fruit (essentially no healthy protein) or some on-the-go bar (extremely little healthy protein). Yet, I quickly understood that the morning meal is just one of the less complicated dishes to load with healthy protein, no matter your nutritional choices.

As a presently ovo-vegetarian, I enjoy making clambered eggs and including additional egg whites to up the healthy protein requirements (2 eggs alone have just 12 grams of healthy protein, and each egg white includes $\sim$ 3.6 grams). No matter my nutritional choices, I regularly fill up my plate with sautéed veggies, like mushrooms, spinach, onion, and sweet potato - these include minimal healthy protein, however, they're nutrient-dense and oh so tasty.

## 2. I have a healthy protein powder that I enjoy... and I simply love it

My most excellent recommendation to anybody looking to boost their healthy protein intake is to locate a sturdy protein powder that you enjoy. Healthy protein powder is one of the most convenient methods to include even more healthy protein to your diet regimen - what's not very easy is discovering one that you like, particularly one with few active ingredients. A shake or smoothie in the early morning or post-workout will normally supply anywhere from 20 to 30 grams of healthy protein, which is vital for muscular tissue fixing and healing, and, for me, it knocks out a big portion of my protein objective.

## 3. I combine reduced healthy protein sources with greater healthy protein sources since it accumulates

Something I needed to come to terms with when I started raising my healthy protein intake was that not every food out there was high in healthy protein. Noticeably, I recognize that initially, I just consumed foods that had one of the most grams of protein per bite proportion: healthy protein powder, eggs, lentils, yogurt, anything that had 10 to 20 grams of protein in it. As you can imagine, that approach stopped quickly as I was consuming significant amounts of the same foods (which was as discouraging as it was tiring).

Rather, I started including smaller sized resources of healthy protein like chia seeds (4 grams per tbsp), hemp seeds (3 grams per tbsp), almond butter (4 grams per tbsp), and pumpkin seeds (10 grams per 1/4 cup) to my dishes. Naturally, I assumed that 4 grams would not make much of a distinction, however, if I include some chia seeds to my shake, a tbsp of hemp hearts to a salad, and munch on some pumpkin seeds, I've would have eaten 17 grams of plant-based healthy protein without attempting it - which absolutely makes a distinction.

## 4. I consume more than one healthy protein resource in each dish

With the healthy protein objectives I have, consuming one healthy protein resource per dish simply isn't sufficient in some cases. Who would the desire to consume 3 cups of black beans in one go?

I additionally like a great lentil Bolognese, or using bean-based pasta to make spicy peanut noodles (to which you can add hemp seeds or edamame for even more healthy protein). In our progressively plant-based world, there are limitless means to incorporate different healthy protein sources, and including even more than one to each dish makes sure that I'm delighted and full, both with the dish and with my healthy protein intake.

## 5. I make protein-filled snacks that suppress my food cravings

I do not consume much milk (and when I do, I attempt to go for goat or lamb milk and cheeses), however, I do like yogurt every once in a while. If you have no problems with milk, Icelandic yogurt is a protein-filled choice, and if you are lactose intolerant, try goat or lamb yogurt; I was unconvinced, yet it is simple and really delicious. I have not found a simple, protein-filled vegan yogurt yet, but I still wish to find one.

At night, when I crave something sweet, I'll blend yogurt with some healthy protein powder to make a kind of healthy protein dessert, and I've had some success at making vegan chickpea cookie dough with recipes found on Pinterest. If neither sounds excellent, I will look at the blogosphere for healthy protein cookies or truffles, and after that, I'd include them to my meal-prep strategy (since if there's a place for anything on meal planning, it is a treat).

Currently, if you have reviewed every one of this and are still upset about plant-based healthy protein, please scroll back to the start. If you are thrilled (fingers crossed that all of you are), check out our overview on how to go plant-based, our plant-based recipes, or try out these lesser-known plant-based healthy protein sources.

# CHAPTER 16: PLANT-BASED MEAT SUBSTITUTES

Generally, it is ideal to steer clear of from artificial meat, yet not all choices are horrible.

When it comes to soy, stay clear from artificial meats made with extremely refined variations, like soy focuses and distinctive soy. All that being stated, a block of natural tofu added to stir fry rather than chicken is an excellent source of healthy protein.

Seitan, on the other hand, is ideal stayed clear of, given that it is primarily composed of wheat healthy protein and is typically very refined.

# THE JACKFRUIT COMPANY

*Jackfruit is... Did you think it was a fruit?*

Jackfruit is excellent for you as it is loaded with fiber, potassium, and various other good-for-your-heart nutrients.

Rather than skipping, try oy one of our favored brand names, the *Jackfruit Company*. Attempt the smoked drew jackfruit or the enchilada jackfruit dish.

## Vegan jackfruit burrito bowl

*Pico de gallo:*

- 2 Roma tomatoes, cored and diced.
- 1 tiny red onion (or 1/4 of a tool one), carefully diced.
- A handful of fresh cilantro leaves, cut.
- Sea salt, to taste.

*Burrito bowl:*

- 1 (10-ounce) tex-mex jackfruit, heated according to package directions.
- 1 (15-ounce) can of black beans, drained and washed.
- 2 cups of prepared wild rice.
- Shredded romaine, to taste.
- Shredded red cabbage, to taste.
- 1 little firm-ripe avocado, peeled and very finely cut.
- Vegan sour cream (optional).
- Warm sauce (optional).

*For the pico de gallo:*

In a bowl, mix the tomatoes, red onion, cilantro, and sea salt. Cool up until it is ready to be combined with the other ingredients (it can be made up to 8 hrs in advance).

In 2 spacious bowls, uniformly separate the pico de gallo, the jackfruit, the black beans, wild rice, romaine, and cabbage. Add to each a little bit of the chopped avocado and drizzle with the sour cream and the warm sauce.

*Nutrition value for serving size:*

Calories: 462 | Total fat: 20 g | Saturated fat: 3 g | Cholesterol: o mg | Sodium: 744 mg | Total carbohydrate: 62 g | Dietary fibers: 13 g | Net carbohydrate: 49 g | Sugars: 20 g | Protein: 13 g

## Vegan BBQ jackfruit pulled 'pork' sandwiches

*Barbeque sauce:*

- 1 1/2 cup of tomato sauce.
- 3 tbsp of tomato paste.
- 1 tbsp of molasses.

- 1/4 cup of coconut sugar (can sub with brownish sugar).
- 2 tsp of apple cider vinegar.
- 1 tbsp of chili powder.
- 1 tsp of onion powder.
- 1 tsp of garlic powder.
- 3/4 tsp of smoked paprika.
- 1/2 tsp of mustard powder.
- 1 tsp of salt.

*Drawn jackfruit*:

- 1 tbsp (15 ml) of olive oil.
- 1 medium onion, cut.
- 2 20 oz canisters of green jackfruit in salted water (not syrup).
- 1 cup of BBQ sauce.
- 1 cup (240 ml) water.
- 1-2 tbsp sriracha or chili paste (optional).
- Salt and pepper to preference.
- 8 gluten-free burger/sandwich buns.

*How to make it*:

*Vegan BBQ sauce*

Add every spice to a tiny bowl or a saucepan and blend the tomato sauce in a pot over low heat. Allow simmering for 10 mins. Any time is right, to be honest, but it needs to rest.

*Drawn jackfruit*

Rinse and drain the jackfruit.
Warm up the oil in a frying pan. When the oil is heated, add the cut onion and cook for 5-7 mins, up until the onion is soft.

Add the rinsed jackfruit, BBQ sauce, and water to the frying pan. Mix well and cover with a lid. Cook on low heat for a minimum of 20 mins, mixing sometimes.

Preheat the oven to 400 ° f/200 ° c, line a cooking tray with cooking parchment, and put it aside for the moment.

Use a potato masher or a spatula to mash the jackfruit, make sure that it looks like drawn pork. If along with salt and pepper, you like some chili paste, you can add it as it is an excellent addition to the dish.

To end the recipe, spread out the drawn jackfruit on the lined cooking sheet in a layer and cook in the oven for 10 mins.

If preferred, mix in the BBQ sauce. Add in your burger buns and offer.

*Nutritional values:*

Calories: 348 | Sodium: 727 mg | Carbohydrates: 80 g | Fiber: 4 g | Sugar: 8 g | Protein: 2 g

# F-ISH

*Components*: carrots, rapeseed oil, apple cider vinegar, liquid smoke, sea salt.

F-ish, a London-based firm, is enthusiastic about preserving the sea and your taste buds. The owner says he was very passionate about sea foods before going vegan. Their floral plant-based salmon is just like the real one.

While F-ish is just offered at pick up stores and online in the UK, they've done a couple of partnerships while taking a trip abroad. Keeping our fingers crossed, we're really hoping that these little containers will get on American grocery stores quickly.

## Sushi without a mat

*Ingredients*:

- Rice.
- 1 cup of white rice (sushi rice if you can).

- 2 cups of water.
- 3 tbsp of rice vinegar
- A glass of wine vinegar.
- 2 tbsp of sugar.
- 1/2 tsp of salt.
- 4 sheets of nori (dried out algae).
- 1 cup sliced of veggies (carrot, cucumber, red pepper, avocado).
- Soy sauce/tamari, marinated ginger, wasabi (optional/for offering).

*How to make it*:

Beginning by preparing your rice. Wash the rice in a mesh filter till your water runs clear.

In the meantime, add vinegar, salt, and sugar to a little pan and cook over medium heat mixing periodically up until the sugar and the salt have liquified. Put in a container and cool in the refrigerator up until rice sets.

As soon as the rice is done, turn off the heat and add the cooled down vinegar blend and mix with a rubber spatula or fork, being careful not to overmix. The rice will result to be damp, however, it will be fine once you heat it. Once it is all set, it should be dry and sticky.

In the meantime, prep your veggies by cutting them right into slices. If they're too big, they will prevent rolling sushi.

When it is time to roll the sushi, get a thick towel, and fold it over right into a rectangular shape and place it on a level surface area. Cover with cling wrap, and after that cover with a sheet of nori. Using your hands dipped in water (to prevent sticking), rub a really slim layer of rice on the nori, seeing to it that it is not too thick, or your roll will be too disproportionated with the filling.

Set up your veggies in a line at the lower 3/4 of the rice closest to you.

Start to roll the nori and the rice over with your fingers, and when the veggies are covered, use the cling wrap and a towel to mold and press the roll. Proceed until it is rolled up.

Cut with a sharp blade and put aside. Offer quickly with marinated ginger, soy sauce, and wasabi.

*Nutritional values:*

Calories: 296 | Fat: 0.5 g | Sodium: 443 mg | Carbohydrates: 62 g | Fiber: 2 g | Sugar: 10 g | Protein: 6 g

# JUST EGGS

*Components:* Water, Mung Bean Protein Isolate, Expeller-Pressed Canola Oil, Less than 2% of seasonings, and all-natural ingredients.

It has long been disputed whether eggs are meat or dairy products. We're still not sure, yet we do know this: a lot of individuals when they first switch to a much more plant-based diet plan, keep consuming eggs. It can be because they like them (even more individuals appear to like the structure and taste of eggs much more so than meat), or it might be since people are afraid they won't get enough healthy protein in their diet plan.

*SIMPLY,* California-based business is the manufacturer of a couple of plant-based foods, consisting of mayo, dressing, cookie dough, and they have refined beef-like produce in their food selections. They likewise make plant-based, non-GMO eggs, 'warm and filling' ones. Perfect for breakfast, cooking, and making vegan fried rice. JUST Eggs shuffle batter measures up to the buzz.

## Morning meal sandwich

*Components:*

- 1/2 cup of JUST Egg.
- 2-3 tsp of oil or butter.
- 3-4 oz of tempeh bacon or bacon.
- 2 brioche buns.
- 2 tbsp of JUST Mayo.
- 2 tbsp of green onions or chives, sliced thin.
- 2 pieces of white cheddar (or comparable sharp white "cheese").
- Warm sauce (optional).

*How to make it:*

*Prepare the bacon or tempeh*

Add a tsp or 2 of butter or oil if you are using the tempeh bacon. Fry the tempeh bacon up until it is well browned and to your preferred degree of crispiness.

*Pan-fry the bread*

Layer each side of the brioche with some JUST Mayo. Place the bread mayo-side down in the very same frying pan over medium heat and fry till the bread is crunchy and browned, using a spatula to push it down gently. Put it aside while you scramble the JUST Egg.

Beat the JUST Egg. Beat like an egg, making sure you allow the JUST Egg to set into curds that will hold well in a morning meal sandwich. Use a tiny, rigid rubber spatula to mix sometimes, while still allowing the JUST Egg to cook uniformly and set.

*Include the green onions*

When the JUST Egg begins to firm, include the green onions (if you favor the taste of the green onions to be stronger, only add them when you have finished assembling the sandwich.) Scumble the mix until the JUST Egg is set, yet not completely dry.

*Construct the sandwich*

Loads the lower side of bread with the warm scrambled mix. Cover the JUST Egg with a piece of cheese, and then with a slice or 2 of bacon. Spread out a little additional JUST Mayo on the top portion of bread, if wanted, and close the sandwich.

*Nutrition value for serving size:*

Calories: 220 | Total fat: 6 g | Saturated fat: 3.5 g | Cholesterol: 15 mg | Sodium: 590 mg | Carbohydrates: 31 g | Net carbs: 30 g | Fiber: 1 g | Glucose: 1 g | Protein: 13 g | Calcium: 150 mg | Iron: 1.2 mg

## French toast

*Components:*

- 8 pieces of hard bread, like a French loaf or brioche (a day old).
- 2 tbsp of sugar.
- 1 tsp of vanilla.
- 1 tsp of cinnamon.
- 1 cup of JUST Egg.
- 1/2 cup of milk (almond creamer is our go-to right here).
- Coconut oil or butter.
- Your preferred garnishes (syrup, berries, powdered sugar...).

*How to make it:*

*Dry the bread*

If your bread is not stale yet, lay it out on a flat pan overnight to completely dry out, or cook it for 10-20 mins in a 300°F oven till it is completely dry and rigid. Using stagnant or dried out bread will aid the absorption of the custard while it prevents the bread from getting floppy.

*Blend the custard*

Blend the JUST Egg, sugar, vanilla, cinnamon and milk in a bread recipe.

*Saturate the bread*

Saturate the bread pieces in the custard mix for 15-30 mins, flipping them after half the time has passed.

*Fry the salute*

Use a fork or tongs to pick up each piece of bread from the bowl, allowing any kind of excess custard blend to drip off back into the bowl. Cook each piece for about 2 mins on each side, up until browned.

*Nutrition value for serving size:*

Calories: 219 | Total fat: 11 g | Saturated fat: 5.2 g | Trans fat: 0.2 g | Polyunsaturated fat: 1.1 g | Cholesterol: 129 mg | Sodium: 237 mg | Potassium: 97 mg | Total carbohydrates: 23 g | Dietary fiber: 1.1 g | Sugars: 4 g | Protein: 7.3 g

# HOMEMADE

It is effortless to replace homemade, whole food options for fake meats in your dishes. While simulated meats can be useful and hassle-free replacements, particularly when you initially go vegan (they give a simple method to switch out vegan choices in a dish, while still consuming food you are acquainted with), they can be pricey and challenging to discover depending where you live.

And while they might be devoid of cholesterol and reduced in hydrogenated fats than meat, even if they're meat-free does not indicate they're great for you. Numerous simulated meats might be harmful, as well. They are, nevertheless, typically refined foods, and depending upon the brand name, they might still have plenty of harmful active ingredients, such as excessive salt.

Do not be afraid, nevertheless, to try to make vegan simulated meat options at home. Have a look at the summary of dishes listed below if you are craving a veggie hamburger, meat, or perhaps a fish and shellfish bake! The majority of them are or could be made soy- and are thus gluten-free.

## Meat-free crumbles

These meat-free vegan crumbles and soy-free too, sound delicious - excellent for those with a soy intolerance! They should be eaten with for pasta, tacos, and pizza. They are made with good-for-you and delicious ingredients like cauliflower and walnuts, and they are quite savory and smoky.

## Vegetable bacon

Make your very own vegetable bacon at your house, it is excellent, has a smoky taste, and it is salty. You can choose its ingredients: you can make it with coconut, eggplant, or mushrooms.

## Homemade seitan

Seitan, or 'wheat meat' has been extensively used in vegan Chinese food for many of years and is a flexible meat alternative that can stand in for beef, duck, or chicken. Make seitan at home so you can eat as much as you desire!

## Vegetable burger

Ah, the essential vegetable choice. The veggie burger is the default veg choice in several dining establishments that you could simply be sick of it by now.

## Chickpea treats

Chickpeas are a fantastic whole-food choice for simulated meats! You can make delicious quinoa-chickpea cakes! You can attempt to make your very own tofu or tempeh.

# CONCLUSIONS

Your hair and nails are practically entirely made of healthy protein, and your body uses healthy protein to construct muscular tissue, to fix cells, and to create enzymes, hormonal agents, and various other crucial biochemicals. What makes healthy protein extra essential is the fact that the body does not save it in the same way it stores fat and carbohydrate - this implies that you require a consistent consumption to fulfill your demands.

Going vegan or vegetarian calls for some preparation. With the best protein-based plant food, nonetheless, individuals that do not eat animal-derived food can consume well-balanced diet plans that sustain a healthy and balanced body and decreases the threats of some illness.

It is necessary to talk about the nutritional parts with a physician or nutritional expert, given that vegan or vegetarian diet plans might not have some crucial nutrients, requiring the consumption of nutritional supplements, or discovering how to find out if a particular food is high in these nutrients.

If you desire to remain healthy and to prevent health diseases, it is ideal to get as many of your healthy protein from plants. You can obtain the healthy protein you need from a range of garden-grown pants every day.

As you might know, there are 5 food groups (veggies, fruits, grains, healthy proteins, milk). They normally count as veggies, and they might additionally certify as healthy proteins.

Usually, people that regularly consume chicken, meat, and fish would put beans and peas in the Vegetable Group, vegetarians, and vegans that rarely consume chicken, fish, or meat would count several of the peas and beans they consume in the Protein Foods Group.

Lightning Source UK Ltd.
Milton Keynes UK
UKHW020654220621
385957UK00009B/406